Motivational Interviewing for African Americans

A Culturally Responsive Guide for Practitioners

Kenneth Ginlack, LCSW, CSAC, ICS

Published: May 31, 2025
ISBN-13: 979-8286047871
ASIN: B0FBZ1VJX7

Motivational Interviewing for African Americans: Deluxe Edition

Written by Kenneth Ginlack, LCSW, CSAC, ICS
Published by Transformed Press

Printed in the United States of America.

ISBN: 979-8-218-72678-2

For more information, visit: www.transformedpress.com

TRANSFORMED
PRESS

Contents

Acknowledgments 1

Foreword 2

Introduction: 4
Why We Need This Manual

1. Understanding Motivational Interviewing (MI) 5
2. Why Culture Matters in Motivational Interviewing 7
3. Stages of Change Through a Cultural Lens 11
4. The Role of the Practitioner 15
5. Core Skills of Motivational Interviewing (OARS) in Black Communities 18
6. Working with Mandated Clients 22
7. Trauma, Mistrust, and Historical Wounds 26
8. The Language of Change in Black Communities 30
9. Addressing Internalized Oppression and Identity in Recovery 34
10. Group Dynamics and Peer Influence 38
11. Spirituality, Legacy, and Healing Beyond the Session 42
12. Cultural Resistance to Treatment and the Power of Reframing 46
13. Reentry, Restoration, and Reclaiming Identity 50
14. Trauma, Truth-Telling, and Healing the Wounds We Don't Name 54
15. In the Black community, healing rarely happens alone 58
16. Peer Support and Mentorship in MI 61

17. Black Men and Vulnerability in the Recovery Space 64
18. Addressing Systemic Racism in the Therapeutic Relationship 68
19. The Role of the Practitioner—Cultural Humility Over Cultural Competence 72
20. Bringing It All Together—Practice, Policy, and Power 76
21. Final Notes 79
22. Acknowledgments II 80
Thank You
23. References 81
24. Appendix A: 82
Sample Affirmations Adapted for African American Clients
25. Appendix B: 84
Sample Reflections Reworded for Cultural Responsiveness
26. Appendix C: 85
Open-ended questions are foundational in Motivational Interviewing
27. Appendix D: 87
Group Guidelines for Culturally Grounded MI Sessions
28. Appendix E: 89
Addressing Common Client Statements with Cultural Sensitivity
29. Appendix F: 91
Practitioner Reflection Prompts for Cultural Self-Awareness
30. About The Author 94

Acknowledgments

Acknowledgments

This manual was made possible through the collective resilience, cultural insight, and unwavering strength of Black individuals and communities who have shaped our understanding of healing and recovery.

To every person who has shared their story, extended their support, or stood in the gap we see you and we thank you.

To the mentors, clinicians, peer supporters, elders, and brothers who have walked this path with me, your wisdom and encouragement gave this work depth and direction.

To my team at Serenity Inns Inc., your belief in culturally responsive care has fueled this journey every step of the way.

Finally, to those still healing, still fighting, and still hoping, this work is for you.

Foreword

"If you want to lift yourself up, lift up someone else."– Booker T. Washington

This manual was born out of necessity—spiritual, clinical, and cultural. For far too long, therapeutic tools have been created for us, but not with us. Motivational Interviewing (MI), while evidence-based and widely used, often misses the mark when it comes to honoring the lived experiences of Black people—especially those navigating trauma, addiction, incarceration, and systemic racism.

What's been missing is voice. Our voice.

This work centers that voice. It weaves together the rigor of MI with the rhythm of our culture, the pain of our histories, and the strength of our communities. It challenges practitioners to approach healing not as a transaction, but as a sacred exchange—a moment to stand in truth, dignity, and restoration with someone who's been told they're too angry, too broken, too far gone.

This is not just a guide. It's a declaration: Black healing is real, necessary, and ours to lead.

Introduction: Why We Need This Manual

For years, I sat in rooms—some as a client, some as a clinician, and others as a leader—and I saw the same thing over and over: Black men and women being handed tools that weren't built for us. Tools that didn't speak our language. Tools that ignored our pain. Tools that missed our brilliance. Tools that treated our survival as resistance instead of resilience.

Motivational Interviewing is one of the most powerful approaches we have in the behavioral health world. But even MI, with all its intention and empathy, often falls short when it's not adapted to our cultural truth.

This manual changes that.

It's for the brother who says, "My PO made me come here. ain't nothing wrong with smoking weed." It's for the woman balancing motherhood and recovery, tired of being judged by people who don't know her fight. It's for the teen who doesn't say much but still shows up. It's for the facilitator, the peer, the clinician, the elder, the pastor—anyone holding space for healing in our communities.

This isn't about reinventing MI. It's about reclaiming it.

Introduction:

Why We Need This Manual

For years, I sat in rooms—some as a client, some as a clinician, and others as a leader—and I saw the same thing over and over: Black men and women being handed tools that weren't built for us. Tools that didn't speak our language. Tools that ignored our pain. Tools that missed our brilliance. Tools that treated our survival as resistance instead of resilience.

Motivational Interviewing is one of the most powerful approaches we have in the behavioral health world. But even MI, with all its intention and empathy, often falls short when it's not adapted to our cultural truth.

This manual changes that.

It's for the brother who says, "My PO made me come here. ain't nothing wrong with smoking weed. "It's for the woman balancing motherhood and recovery, tired of being judged by people who don't know her fight.It's for the teen who doesn't say much but still shows up.It's for the facilitator, the peer, the clinician, the elder, the pastor—anyone holding space for healing in our communities.

This isn't about reinventing MI. It's about reclaiming it.

Chapter 1
Understanding Motivational Interviewing (MI)

When people walk into a recovery program, a peer group, or a counseling session, they don't always walk in ready to change. They come in with pain, with questions, and with pressure—from their PO, from their family, from the courts, or from the streets. What Motivational Interviewing offers is a way to meet that person exactly where they are, without force, without shame, and without assumptions.

Motivational Interviewing, or MI, is a counseling style developed by Drs. William Miller and Stephen Rollnick. At its core, MI is a collaborative conversation style that helps people resolve ambivalence and find their own motivation for change. It's not about convincing someone to do what you want them to do. It's about helping them discover what they want to do—and why.

This approach is especially powerful in addiction treatment, reentry programs, and behavioral health services where people are often in stages of readiness that fluctuate day to day. MI is based on the belief that change is more likely to happen when it's self-directed, when the motivation comes from within, not from outside pressure.

That's where the real strength of MI lies. It respects the client's autonomy. It assumes that every person already has within them the ability to change, and that our role as practitioners is not to fix them, but to walk alongside them, listen deeply, and help them reconnect to their values, goals, and strengths.

The Four Processes of MI

To understand MI deeply, we have to look at its four core processes:

Engaging – Building a trusting and respectful relationship. Without trust, no real work happens.

Focusing – Helping the person narrow down the conversation to a specific goal or behavior they're thinking about changing.

Evoking – Drawing out the person's own reasons for change. This is the heart of MI. It's about listening for what matters to them.

Planning – Once someone feels ready, you help them develop a plan that fits their life, values, and situation.

Each of these processes builds on the one before it. If at any point the conversation feels forced or rushed, we return to engagement. MI is flexible. It follows the person, not a script.

The Spirit of MI

Chapter 2
Why Culture Matters in Motivational Interviewing

Motivational Interviewing was developed with a universal spirit in mind, but it was not created within a culturally specific context. That's important to say at the beginning of this chapter, because when a tool is assumed to work the same for everyone, it risks working well for no one. Culture shapes how we listen, how we speak, how we express emotion, and how we build trust. For African Americans, culture is not just background, it's survival.

You cannot separate a person's readiness to change from their lived experience. You cannot expect someone to open up in a counseling session when everything about the room – from the walls, to the questions – feels foreign, clinical, or cold. For Black clients, particularly those who've been criminalized, marginalized, or pathologized, that feeling isn't just discomfort, it's a warning sign.

Why Cultural Adaptation Is Essential

Cultural adaptation in Motivational Interviewing is not about changing the core values of MI, it's about honoring the core values of the client.

That includes:

Their communication style,

Their historical experience with systems,

Their family and community dynamics,

Their worldview and spiritual beliefs,

Their understanding of power and authority.

When these are ignored, practitioners unintentionally reinforce the very dynamics MI seeks to dismantle – power over the client, disconnection from their own voice, and externally imposed goals.

When these are respected, MI becomes a culturally resonant tool, one that not only promotes behavior change, but restores dignity in the process.

The African American Experience in Clinical Spaces

To understand how MI can be adapted, we must first understand the barriers Black clients face when entering behavioral health services.

Some of those barriers include:

Historical mistrust of institutions, due to unethical medical practices (like the Tuskegee Syphilis Study) and systemic neglect.

Criminal legal system involvement, where treatment is often mandated, not chosen.

Bias in diagnosis and treatment, with Black clients more likely to be labeled with severe or stigmatized disorders.

Stigma in the community, where asking for help can be seen as weakness.

Over-surveillance and under-support, especially for Black men.

These experiences shape how a person hears a question, how they interpret a tone of voice, and whether they believe they are being judged or respected.

Respecting Communication Styles

African American communication styles are deeply rooted in history, spirituality, music, rhythm, and storytelling. They are often animated, metaphorical, and filled with emotion. That's not resistance, that's cultural fluency.

In many clinical environments, especially when using MI, providers are trained to remain neutral, calm, and still. But neutrality without warmth reads as cold. Stillness without response reads as disinterest. "Professionalism, " when not culturally attuned, can feel like distance.

A culturally responsive MI practitioner mirrors tone with care, uses rhythm and language that matches the client, and doesn't fear passion or volume. When a client is expressive, that's not an invitation to redirect, it's a doorway to deepen the connection.

Trauma and Cultural Memory

Many Black clients carry the weight of generational trauma, whether they name it or not. That trauma shows up in the body, in language, and in silence. MI gives us a way to sit with that trauma and not flinch. But we must be willing to recognize its form.

That client who won't make eye contact? They've been trained not to.

The man who laughs after sharing something painful? He's masking grief with humor.

The woman who looks "angry" in group? She's protecting her vulnerability.

MI, when culturally informed, sees beyond the surface. It reads the emotion underneath, and reflects that emotion with honesty and care.

Avoiding Cultural Errors in MI

Here are some common mistakes well-meaning practitioners make when delivering MI in Black communities:

Over-paraphrasing: Repeating the client's words with too much polish or detachment can feel like mimicry or judgment.

Overusing reflections: Too many reflections, especially if formulaic, can sound robotic or fake.

Under-affirming: Avoiding direct praise for fear of "bias" leads to missed opportunities to reinforce strength.

Ignoring identity: Failing to acknowledge the client's race, gender, or lived experience disconnects the conversation from reality.

Practicing MI across cultures means seeing the full person, not just the presenting behavior. It means listening to more than words, it means listening to story, rhythm, and silence.

Bringing MI into the Culture, Not the Other Way Around

We are not asking our clients to fit into MI. We are bringing MI into their world.

That means:

Reframing how we ask questions,

Shifting our tone,

Allowing emotion,

Acknowledging pain without pathologizing it.

It also means recognizing when the client is the expert in the room. MI tells us to draw out the client's wisdom, but in Black communities, that wisdom often comes in forms we weren't trained to see. It comes through coded language, through side comments, through body language, through spirit.

When we listen with cultural ears, we hear the deeper story.

Closing Reflection

Culture isn't something we "include" in Motivational Interviewing. It's something we start with. It's the foundation, not the detail.

For Black clients, healing doesn't happen in a vacuum. It happens in context. It happens when someone sees you – not just as a person in treatment, but as a person with history, with pride, with scars, and with purpose.

This is why we do this work. And this is where the change begins.

Chapter 3

Stages of Change Through a Cultural Lens

Motivational Interviewing is grounded in the idea that people change in stages. Nobody flips a switch overnight. We move forward, we step back, we hesitate, we test the waters. The Stages of Change model, also known as the Transtheoretical Model, helps us understand that process.

But to make this model truly effective with African American clients, we must look at it through a cultural lens. The road to change for our people is not always about internal readiness. Sometimes, it's about surviving the system long enough to believe that change is even possible.

The Six Stages of Change

The model identifies six stages:

Precontemplation – "I don't have a problem."

Contemplation – "Maybe I have a problem."

Preparation – "I want to do something about this."

Action – "I'm doing something about it."

Maintenance – "I'm working to keep the change going."

Relapse – "I slipped, but I'm not starting from scratch."

Each stage represents a point along the journey, not a permanent identity. The job of the practitioner is to meet the client where they are, not where we think they should be.

Precontemplation: "I Don't Have a Problem"

In traditional MI, this stage is seen as denial. But for many Black clients, what looks like denial is actually protection.

A young man on probation who says, "Weed isn't a problem, my PO is," isn't avoiding the truth. He's responding to a system that criminalized him before it ever offered him help.

In this stage, your role is not to argue or confront. It's to listen, affirm, and gently invite exploration. Reflect their values, not just their words. Say things like:

"You've had a lot of people telling you what's wrong with you. I'm here to understand what's right about you."

We honor the resistance, not fight it.

Contemplation: "Maybe There's a Problem"

This is where ambivalence lives. A client may say, "I don't know, I feel better when I use, but I'm tired of getting locked up."

This inner conflict is not a barrier—it's the beginning of movement. But culturally, it can be complicated by pride, survival instincts, and fear of being vulnerable.

Help the client see both sides of the coin. Ask open-ended questions like:

"What are the things you like about using? And what are the things that are getting in the way?"

Avoid judging. Validate both the struggle and the strength it takes to admit the struggle.

Preparation: "I'm Ready to Try"

When clients begin to say, "I need to do something different," they're stepping into possibility.

But here's where cultural factors matter. Black clients preparing for change often don't have the same resources or support systems. Transportation, childcare, safe housing, and financial instability can all delay action.

Don't assume readiness means the same thing for everyone. Preparation may look like a small shift, changing who they hang out with, thinking about detox, or showing up to group more often.

Affirm their momentum:

"You've already made some changes just by thinking and showing up. That tells me something about you."

Action: "I'm Doing It"

In this stage, the client is actively changing. They may be in treatment, attending support groups, reconnecting with family, or staying away from triggers.

Support in this phase means walking with them, not just watching. Reinforce their progress without over-praising. Culturally, many Black clients are uncomfortable with being "talked down to" even when it's meant as encouragement. Stay grounded, and celebrate with humility.

Ask:

"What's been helping you stay focused? What strengths are you noticing in yourself?"

Don't just talk about behavior talk about identity.

Maintenance: "I'm Holding On"

Maintenance is where real recovery builds. But it's also where systems tend to step away, probation ends, the program ends, and suddenly the support disappears.

For African Americans, especially those with few safety nets, this is when isolation, stress, and racism can re-emerge as powerful triggers.

Support clients in building culturally meaningful routines. That might mean reconnecting with the Black church, mentoring others, joining community groups, or creating their own recovery practices.

Say:

"What keeps you going when no one's watching? Who helps you remember who you are?"

Help them shift from surviving to thriving.

Relapse: "I Slipped"

Relapse is not failure. It's a common part of the cycle of change. But for many Black clients, a slip doesn't just mean starting over it can mean jail, shame, or re-traumatization.

Approach this moment with compassion. Say:

"This doesn't erase all the work you've done. What did you learn from it?"

Use MI to explore the meaning behind the lapse. Was it stress? Isolation? Hopelessness? Then, together, rebuild a plan with respect and dignity.

Cultural Notes for All Stages

Throughout all six stages, practitioners must stay aware of the cultural messages Black clients receive from the world around them:

"You're dangerous."

"You're hopeless."

"You're too angry."

"You're too broken to fix."

MI gives us a way to fight those lies. To say instead:

"You have value."

"You know what's best for you."

"You're allowed to take your time."

"You don't have to do this alone."

When we apply the Stages of Change with cultural awareness, we're not just promoting recovery. We're restoring identity.

Chapter 4
The Role of the Practitioner

Motivational Interviewing is only as powerful as the person delivering it. The tools are important, but the person holding them matters more. A hammer can build or destroy depending on the hands that use it. The same is true with MI. The role of the practitioner is not just to guide change it is to create a space where change becomes possible.

In working with African American clients, the practitioner's role expands beyond the clinical. You become a witness, a listener, a challenger, a mirror, and sometimes even a surrogate source of trust in a system that has broken it.

More Than a Skill Set

MI is not something you do to people it's a way of being with them. This is especially true when working with communities that have experienced harm at the hands of systems. Your presence, tone, timing, and transparency matter. People don't just hear your words they read your energy.

In African American culture, communication is layered. We notice body language, side glances, the pause before a question, the silence after a reflection. Clients will pick up on inauthenticity. If you're not real, they'll know. If you're just following a script, they'll feel it.

Practitioners must show up fully human, fully engaged, and fully humble.

Building Trust Without Pretending to "Know"

One of the biggest mistakes practitioners make especially white practitioners or those unfamiliar with the Black experience is rushing to show that they understand. Sometimes, that comes from a good place. But it often lands as forced, performative, or worse insulting.

Trust doesn't come from saying "I get it." It comes from showing respect without needing to prove yourself.

You build trust by:

Being consistent

Listening more than you talk

Reflecting without judgment

Owning your blind spots

Not avoiding race or culture when it's clearly in the room

Say things like:

"I can't pretend to know your experience, but I want to understand what this has meant for you."

Or:

"You don't have to explain everything. I'm here to listen, not to fix."

Let the client lead the depth of disclosure. Your job is to hold space, not dig.

Using Your Power Responsibly

Whether you are a peer mentor, a therapist, a case worker, or a group facilitator, you hold power. That power can heal or harm. African American clients have often had their autonomy stripped—from schools, the justice system, the workplace, even within the medical field.

When you walk into a room with a clipboard, a treatment plan, or control over someone's next steps, you're representing a system. You can either repeat the trauma of that system, or you can disrupt it.

Disruption doesn't mean being passive. It means choosing partnership over authority. It means asking, not telling. It means checking in before challenging. It means not assuming readiness because someone showed up in your office.

Ask permission before giving advice:

"Would it be okay if I shared a thought with you?"

Ask before reflecting sensitive emotions:

"Can I reflect something I heard, and you tell me if I'm off?"

Small moments of respect build long-term trust.

Emotional Presence and Cultural Competency

Cultural competency is not knowing everything about a group. It's knowing that you don't. It's the willingness to listen to how someone's identity shapes their experience of change. Emotional presence means not flinching when someone shares pain. It means not retreating when the conversation gets uncomfortable.

In MI, we use the term "accurate empathy." But in Black communities, accuracy comes from attunement. It's less about getting the words perfect, and more about being real.

When someone says, "I'm tired of this shit," don't respond with, "It sounds like you're feeling frustrated." That sounds like therapy talk. Instead, you might say:

"Yeah, it sounds like this is wearing you down."

Match energy with respect. Speak like a person, not a provider.

Self-Reflection for Practitioners

To use MI with cultural humility, you must know yourself. Ask:

What biases do I carry into this room?

Where do I feel the urge to control?

What emotions do I avoid when clients express them?

How do I respond when race is named?

Am I here to feel needed, or to support growth?

Your self-awareness is your tool. It keeps your MI grounded in authenticity, not performance.

Representing Healing in Real Time

In many cases, you may be the first person to ever give a client room to think, to talk, to process without punishment. That is sacred work.

When you sit across from someone and truly listen, you're not just helping them change a behavior you're giving them a new experience of being seen.

This is the heart of MI. Not the techniques, not the acronym, not the steps. The presence. The respect. The belief that the client is already whole and capable.

When you hold that belief consistently, even when the client doesn't believe it for themselves that's when change begins.

Chapter 5
Core Skills of Motivational Interviewing (OARS) in Black Communities

Motivational Interviewing uses four foundational skills, known by the acronym OARS: Open-ended questions, Affirmations, Reflections, and Summaries. These tools are simple, but they are powerful when used with intention, cultural sensitivity, and genuine presence. In African American communities, how we use these tools matters just as much as when we use them.

For many Black clients, the clinical world can feel foreign, disconnected, or even condescending. That means every question, every reflection, every moment of silence—carries weight. OARS is not just about helping clients talk. It's about showing clients that we know how to listen.

Open-Ended Questions

Open-ended questions invite clients to speak freely. Instead of leading them down a yes-or-no path, we allow them to define what matters most to them. But not all open-ended questions land the same way in Black spaces. A question that sounds curious to one person may sound like interrogation to another.

Avoid:

"What do you think your problem is?"

Try instead:

"What's been going on in your world lately?""When you think about change, what comes to mind first?""What do you want more of in your life?"

Tone matters. Openness isn't just about grammar. It's about energy. If the question feels like a trap or sounds rehearsed, it won't build trust. Ask from a place of humility, not control.

When you ask a question, give the client space. Don't rush to fill the silence. Many Black clients have been cut off, dismissed, or redirected their entire lives. Let your silence be a signal that you actually want to hear them.

Affirmations

Affirmations are not compliments. They're recognitions of strength. In Black communities, where strength has often been a matter of survival, affirmations carry deep power when they are genuine and specific.

But practitioners often get this wrong. Either they avoid affirming out of fear of overstepping, or they overdo it with generic praise that feels shallow or performative.

Avoid:

"You're awesome."

Try instead:

"It took a lot of strength to walk through that door today.""You've been holding down a lot, and you're still showing up.""That choice you made tells me you're thinking deeply about your next steps."

Affirming someone in a real way means seeing them—not for what they've done wrong, but for how they've survived, adapted, resisted, and grown. It means not assuming that quiet means disengaged or that anger means defiant. It means honoring the ways Black people have had to carry pain without breaking.

Affirmation becomes healing when it speaks to identity, not just behavior.

Reflections

Reflections are a key part of MI. They show the client that you're listening, that you understand, and that you're tracking their internal process. But when reflections are too clinical or too literal, they can miss the mark, especially in Black communities where language is layered with rhythm, emotion, and nuance.

A client might say:

"I'm tired of the system always trying to put me in a box."

A robotic reflection would be:

"You feel tired of being put in a box."

That's technically correct, but it's not relational. It doesn't match the tone or the emotional truth.

A better reflection might be:

"You've been dealing with this for so long, and it feels like no matter what you do, someone's still trying to label you."

That kind of reflection shows cultural listening. It picks up on the feeling beneath the words and reflects it in a way that honors the speaker.

Another key: Don't overuse reflections. Too many reflections in a row can feel unnatural or like a test. Mix in affirmations, questions, silence. Let the conversation breathe.

Summaries

Summaries in MI are used to gather what's been said, highlight ambivalence, or transition to a new topic. They help the client hear their own thoughts more clearly.

In Black spaces, summaries can be especially helpful when clients are processing complex emotions, shifting between hope and frustration, or trying to make sense of conflicting motivations.

But here's the thing: don't just summarize what was said. Summarize what was felt.

Instead of:

"So you said you're tired of court, you want to stop using, but you don't trust rehab."

Try:

"What I'm hearing is that you're worn out by the system, and even though you want something better, it's hard to believe anything out there will actually help."

When done right, summaries can validate and empower. They say, "I've been listening closely," and they help the client hear their own story in a new way.

OARS in Rhythm With Culture

OARS is a framework, not a script. In Black communities, where conversation is often rich with storytelling, body language, metaphor, and tone, OARS must move in rhythm. That means adapting your approach without changing your intention.

It's okay to sound like yourself. In fact, it's necessary. Don't try to imitate how someone else uses MI. Don't strip your voice of feeling. Speak in a way that connects—because connection is the heart of Motivational Interviewing.

Practicing OARS with cultural humility means:

Listening with your full body.

Mirroring energy, not just words.

Making room for anger, grief, joy, and hope.

Being quiet when needed.

Being real at all times.

Closing Reflection

The tools of Motivational Interviewing are not magic on their own. But in the hands of a culturally attuned, present, and respectful practitioner, they can open doors to transformation.

In African American communities, OARS becomes more than a method. It becomes a ministry of listening, a rhythm of respect, a way to help people remember their power and reclaim their path.

When used with care, these four tools do more than motivate. They heal.

Chapter 6
Working with Mandated Clients

Many African American clients enter treatment not because they want to, but because someone else made them. It may be a probation officer, a judge, child protective services, or an employer. These are what we call mandated clients, and they show up with one message playing loud in their heads:

"I don't want to be here."

Practitioners often make the mistake of labeling these clients as resistant, unmotivated, or non-compliant. But what if we shifted the lens? What if we started with this truth: mandated clients aren't resistant to change they're resistant to control.

When you've spent your life being told what to do, when to eat, where to go, and how to act—being "referred" to treatment feels like just another form of surveillance. That is especially true for Black men who've been in and out of courtrooms, jail cells, and mandated programs that never actually heard their voice.

Motivational Interviewing offers a different way.

"I'm Only Here So I Don't Go Back to Jail"

We've all heard this line. Sometimes it's said with defiance, sometimes with exhaustion. Either way, it's not a refusal to engage it's a protective shield. When someone says this, they're often really saying:

"This system has never helped me before, why should I trust it now?"

In these moments, MI teaches us to lean in, not push back. You don't argue with that statement. You reflect it.

"So right now, the only reason you're here is to avoid more legal trouble."

Then pause. Let them sit with that. That pause is not an ending it's an opening. If the client trusts your tone and believes you're not judging them, they will often keep talking. And in what they say next, you'll begin to hear what really matters to them.

Shifting from Compliance to Connection

Mandated clients are experts at "telling you what you want to hear." They've learned how to pass urine screens, say the right words in group, and fake insight when necessary. This is not manipulation—it's survival. It's what happens when people are forced into spaces that don't feel safe.

Your job is not to force honesty it's to create a space where honesty can feel safe again.

Ask questions like:

"What's something you wish people in programs actually understood?"

"If you could change one thing about how these systems treat you, what would it be?"

"What's something important to you that has nothing to do with court?"

These questions invite dignity. They remind the client that they are more than a case number, more than a referral, more than a checkbox.

Addressing Power Dynamics Directly

If the client feels like you're "just another part of the system," they will hold back. That's normal. What's different about MI is that you don't pretend that power doesn't exist. You name it, and then you give some of it back.

You can say:

"You didn't choose to be here, and that probably affects how open you feel like being. I respect that, and I want to work with you in a way that feels real, not forced."

This kind of honesty disarms defenses. It shows that you're not there to control them you're there to support them. Even if you still have to report progress to a PO or follow program rules, your tone and approach can still communicate partnership.

Finding the Client's Voice

One of the most powerful things MI can do for a mandated client is to help them find their own voice again. The world has been loud about who they are. MI gives them a chance to speak for themselves.

Use affirmations to reinforce their self-awareness:

"You've been clear about what's real for you, and that honesty takes strength."

Use reflections to deepen trust:

"You've done a lot of things because you had to, not because you believed in them. That's exhausting."

And most importantly, listen for change talk no matter how small.

If a client says, "I mean, I don't want to die using," that's not resistance. That's hope peeking through. Reflect it back.

"Even though you don't trust this process, there's part of you that wants something different."

That reflection isn't just technique it's validation. And in that moment, the work begins.

When Clients Don't Talk

Sometimes, the silence in the room feels heavy. The client may shrug, look at their phone, or just sit there. This is where MI asks us to be patient. Don't lecture. Don't guilt them. And don't confuse silence with apathy.

Try saying:

"I'm not here to force anything. You're in the driver's seat. If there's something you want to talk about related to this or not I'm open."

That may sound too relaxed for some providers. But for mandated clients, especially Black men who are used to being told what to do, this approach often opens the door.

If nothing else, they'll remember you didn't treat them like an inmate or a number. That matters.

Cultural Considerations with Mandated Clients

For African American clients, mandated treatment often feels like punishment disguised as help. To undo that harm, practitioners must be deeply aware of how culture and history impact trust.

Don't pathologize anger it may be the most honest emotion in the room.

Don't expect vulnerability right away it has to be earned.

Don't assume progress looks the same for everyone showing up is progress.

The more culturally grounded your approach, the more you help the client see treatment as something they can own not just something they must endure.

Closing Reflection

Working with mandated clients is not about fixing attitudes. It's about shifting relationships from power to partnership, from silence to voice, from survival to self-determination.

When Motivational Interviewing is done with cultural humility and genuine presence, even the most guarded client can begin to open up not because they were told to, but because someone finally made space for them to be human.

Chapter 7
Trauma, Mistrust, and Historical Wounds

You cannot effectively use Motivational Interviewing in African American communities without understanding trauma. Not just individual trauma but historical trauma, racial trauma, and the collective pain passed down through generations.

Too often, practitioners treat trauma like a moment. In our communities, trauma is a context. It's the air many of us have breathed since birth. It's the tension in the shoulders, the double takes in the rearview mirror, the heartbreak of being treated as less than. It doesn't start or stop with a single event.

This chapter explores how trauma, mistrust, and history shape the way Black clients engage in Motivational Interviewing and how practitioners can show up in a way that honors those realities.

Layers of Trauma

For many Black clients, trauma lives in layers:

Personal trauma: abuse, violence, loss, betrayal, incarceration

Community trauma: gun violence, policing, poverty, displacement

Historical trauma: slavery, Jim Crow, redlining, mass incarceration

Vicarious trauma: witnessing injustice through media, social networks, and family narratives

These layers don't just affect the past they shape how people respond in the present. That includes how they respond to treatment, to authority, and to change.

MI must recognize these layers. A client's guardedness is not just resistance, it may be protection from a world that hasn't felt safe. A client's silence may not mean they don't care—it may mean they've learned that silence is safer than vulnerability.

"White People Always Think They Know What's Best for Black People"

A client once said this in a group, and it stopped the room cold. Not because it was offensive but because it was true.

For too long, treatment approaches have centered white cultural norms. Clients are told what "normal" looks like, what "health" sounds like, what "success" means. And when Black clients don't conform, the system labels them as resistant, oppositional, or unmotivated.

MI offers a chance to shift that dynamic. But only if the practitioner is willing to step back from being the expert and lean in to being a learner.

When a client says, "White people always think they know what's best," don't defend yourself. Don't deflect. Instead, reflect.

"It sounds like a lot of people have come into your life thinking they knew better than you and that left you feeling disrespected."

That kind of reflection shows humility. It tells the client, "I hear you," not "Let me fix you." And that creates space for healing.

Anger, Pain, and Survival

Practitioners often avoid clients who express anger. But in Black communities, anger is often a survival tool. It's not always about aggression—it's about protection.

A client who says, "My cousin got shot last night, so f*** this group right now," isn't being disrespectful. They're expressing grief. They're saying, "My world is falling apart, and I don't feel safe here."

In those moments, MI requires presence, not performance.

You can say:

"You've got a lot on your heart right now. I don't expect you to be focused on this group with everything going on."

That kind of response honors the pain without trying to control it.

Never pathologize normal responses to abnormal conditions. Validate the emotion. Create space for it. And when the moment is right, invite reflection:

"What do you need most right now?""Is there anything I can do to support you?"

Even if the client walks out, they'll remember that you treated them like a human being.

Rebuilding Trust in Systems That Harmed Us

Many Black clients enter treatment already suspicious of the process. And they have every reason to be.

They've seen people overmedicated instead of heard.

They've watched loved ones arrested instead of supported.

They've experienced treatment as a condition of probation, not a pathway to healing.

Trust, in this context, is not built with credentials or titles. It's built through consistency, honesty, and respect.

To rebuild trust:

Be transparent about your role.

Admit when you don't know something.

Don't hide behind "professionalism" to avoid hard conversations.

Make room for conversations about race, power, and identity.

You don't have to be perfect. You have to be present.

Trauma-Informed MI in Black Communities

Motivational Interviewing is already trauma-informed at its core. But in Black communities, it must go further. It must recognize that trauma is not the exception it's often the starting point.

This means:

Asking permission before reflecting deep pain

Slowing down the pace when clients seem overwhelmed

Letting go of rigid treatment agendas

Prioritizing the client's sense of safety over the agency's timeline

It also means being willing to sit in discomfort. To hear the rage. To witness the grief. To validate the strength that comes from surviving systems that were not built to support us.

Closing Reflection

Trauma in Black communities is real, layered, and ongoing. But so is resilience. So is wisdom. So is the sacred ability to transform pain into purpose.

Motivational Interviewing, when used with cultural humility and deep emotional presence, doesn't just help clients change it helps them heal.

As practitioners, our role is not to fix trauma. It is to create space where clients feel strong enough to face it and powerful enough to move forward.

Chapter 8

The Language of Change in Black Communities

In Motivational Interviewing, we are taught to listen for "change talk"—the client's own language that signals a desire, ability, reason, or need to change. But if you're not listening with cultural ears, you might miss it. In African American communities, change talk doesn't always sound like it does in a textbook.

It might sound like:

"I'm tired of running." "I can't keep living like this." "They waiting for me to mess up but I ain't giving them that satisfaction."

These are not passive statements. They're declarations of hope buried in frustration. They're survival wisdom wrapped in guarded speech. They're the client's way of saying, "Something's gotta give," even if they're not sure what that is yet.

The language of change in our communities is rich, emotional, spiritual, and coded. If you don't know how to hear it, you'll think nothing is happening. If you do know how to hear it, you'll understand that the healing has already begun.

How We Speak Reflects How We've Survived

Black communication is dynamic. It is shaped by history, rhythm, improvisation, storytelling, and cultural rules that go beyond words. We have learned to speak in code, to read between lines, to say things without saying them. This is not avoidance—it's protection.

When working with African American clients, change talk often comes in tones, metaphors, and even sarcasm.

Client says:

"I mean, I'm not tryna die out here, but you know, it is what it is."

Underneath that? Ambivalence. Fear. Desire for something better.

MI trains us to listen for "DARN-CAT" statements:

Desire: I want to...

Ability: I can...

Reason: I should...

Need: I have to...

Commitment: I will...

Activation: I'm ready to...

Taking steps: I started to...

But in Black communities, these often come with different energy:

"If I don't switch up, I ain't gon' make it." (Need)"I could get this job if I just stop tripping." (Ability)"I already cut some people off." (Taking steps)

To truly honor the client's process, we must hear what's being said even when it's not said plainly.

When Change Talk Sounds Like Resistance

Sometimes change talk hides inside what sounds like defiance.

Client says:

"My PO made me come here. I don't need no damn help."

That might sound like resistance but what if we reflected the meaning beneath it?

"You're feeling forced into this, and it's hard to trust that it's really for your benefit."

Now the door is open.

Or a client says:

"ain't nobody out here looking out for me, so why should I care?"

You could reflect:

"It's been a long time since you felt like anyone was really in your corner."

The truth is, even the most hostile statements often carry a hidden hope. People don't get loud about things they've given up on completely. That edge in their voice? It means they still care. That sarcasm? It's masking hurt.

Your job is to help uncover the meaning and reflect it back with respect.

Affirming Strength in the Language of Survival

Change talk in Black communities is often laced with strength—even when the words sound unsure.

Client says:

"I'm tryna do better, but it's hard when you've been doing the same shit for years."

Affirm that.

"Even recognizing the need to do better—and showing up here—is already something different."

Affirmation helps translate change talk into self-belief. It gives weight to small steps. It reinforces that even naming the struggle is an act of change.

We don't wait until a client completes a program to affirm growth. We affirm them for speaking their truth, for surviving, for imagining something different.

The Role of Tone and Rhythm

In MI, we are trained to listen for what is said. But in Black communities, how it's said often carries the deeper message.

A pause might mean uncertainty.

Repetition might signal urgency.

A side glance might mean, "Are you actually listening to me?"

A shift in tone might mean you touched a nerve.

This means practitioners must go beyond listening for content. You must become attuned to delivery, presence, body language, and emotional shifts.

When a client leans in, drops their voice, or speaks from their gut—you're not just hearing words. You're witnessing a moment of truth. That is sacred.

Don't interrupt. Don't analyze it. Just hold the space and reflect it back.

"That felt important just now."

Sometimes, that's all it takes to keep the door open.

Recognizing Commitment Without Forcing It

Change talk isn't a guarantee that someone is ready. But it is a signal that they are thinking. Our job is not to rush clients into action. It's to help them explore what their own language means to them.

Use reflections to highlight their ambivalence:

"Part of you wants to stop, and part of you still feels pulled toward that old life."

Use summaries to connect their dots:

"You've talked about wanting to be there for your kids, feeling tired of the hustle, and not trusting this process. That's a lot to hold at once."

When a client hears their own words reflected with clarity, they begin to recognize their own wisdom. They begin to hear themselves differently.

That is when change becomes possible.

Closing Reflection

The language of change in African American communities is layered, poetic, guarded, and bold. It comes from a place of pain, yes—but also from a place of deep strength and vision.

As practitioners, we must train ourselves to hear beyond the words. To listen for the rhythm of the soul behind the sentence. To reflect truth, not textbook.

When we do this well, we don't just help people change—we help them hear themselves more clearly than they ever have before.

Chapter 9
Addressing Internalized Oppression and Identity in Recovery

For many African Americans in recovery, the biggest fight isn't just against addiction it's against the messages we've internalized about who we are, what we're worth, and what we're capable of becoming.

This is the battle of internalized oppression. It's what happens when society tells you you're less than, and over time, part of you starts to believe it.

Motivational Interviewing must make space for this battle. Because if we are only addressing behavior drinking, using, violating probation but we're not addressing shame, racialized trauma, and identity wounds, then we're not really helping people heal.

This chapter explores how to use MI to affirm Black identity, interrupt internalized oppression, and reconnect clients to their power.

What Is Internalized Oppression?

Internalized oppression is the set of beliefs we absorb from systemic racism and social conditioning. It sounds like:

"I ain't never gonna be nothing but a felon.""I ain't smart enough for that job.""People like me don't change.""All I've seen is pain why should I expect joy?"

These aren't just thoughts. They are deep, ingrained narratives shaped by centuries of exclusion, criminalization, and dehumanization. They show up in how Black clients view themselves, their future, and their worthiness of recovery.

You Can't Motivate Someone Who Feels Invisible

One of the biggest mistakes providers make is trying to motivate change in someone who hasn't been seen first. If a client feels invisible, unwanted, or unworthy, telling them to "believe in themselves" won't do anything.

You have to start by seeing them.

"I hear that you've been carrying a lot and it sounds like some part of you started to believe you were supposed to."

"You've survived so much, and I wonder if sometimes that survival made it hard to believe you deserve peace."

Statements like this do more than build rapport. They speak directly to the identity wound. They challenge the lie that says, "You are broken beyond repair."

Shame as a Barrier to Change

In many Black clients, shame shows up as self-blame, withdrawal, or anger. It says, "I messed up too bad to ever get right." It says, "Why bother?" Shame keeps people stuck, not because they don't want to change but because they believe they don't deserve to.

MI doesn't confront shame directly. It surrounds it with compassion.

Use affirmations that affirm worth:

"You're not where you want to be, but you showed up today. That says something about who you are."

Use reflections that reframe failure:

"You've had setbacks, but you've also kept getting back up. That's resilience."

We don't erase shame with slogans. We undo it slowly, with empathy, patience, and truth-telling.

The Impact of "Respectability" Pressure

Some Black clients may overperform, speak in "code-switch," or suppress emotion because they've been taught that respectability is their only path to acceptance.

MI helps us recognize when someone is performing versus when they are being real. And it allows us to gently invite authenticity.

"You don't have to say what you think I want to hear. I'm more interested in what's real for you."

That sentence can be freeing. It tells the client: You don't have to prove your worth here. You already have it.

Recovery is not about becoming acceptable. It's about becoming whole.

Naming Racial Identity Without Making It "About Race"

Some providers hesitate to talk about race or culture because they don't want to "make it about race." But in Black communities, not naming race is often a sign of avoidance—not respect.

You can say:

"Can I ask, how does your experience as a Black man (or woman, or person) shape how you view recovery?"

Or:

"Does your identity play a role in how you've been treated in systems like this one?"

These aren't political questions. They're personal. They make room for truth. And truth is what Motivational Interviewing is all about.

Reclaiming Identity Through the Change Process

Motivational Interviewing supports identity reclamation by giving clients space to define their own values, their own goals, their own voice.

Client says:

"I'm tired of being seen as just another addict."

You reflect:

"You want to be seen as more than your struggle—because you are."

Client says:

"I want my kids to see a different version of me."

You affirm:

"That vision you're holding that's a powerful reason to keep going."

Recovery isn't just about sobriety. It's about identity. And when we help clients reconnect with who they really are—outside of pain, outside of systems, outside of stereotypes—we help them reclaim a future that's been waiting for them.

Closing Reflection

Internalized oppression is heavy. But it's not permanent. Every session, every reflection, every honest conversation is a chance to lift a piece of that weight.

As practitioners, our role is not to force clients to believe in themselves. It's to hold up a mirror and show them the beauty, brilliance, and strength that the world tried to erase.

Motivational Interviewing, in this context, becomes more than a method it becomes a radical act of restoration.

Chapter 10
Group Dynamics and Peer Influence

Group work is a cornerstone of many recovery programs, but for Black clients especially Black men it can be complicated terrain. In group, you're not just navigating the topic at hand. You're navigating status, trust, pride, pain, and survival, all in a room with people who may have walked the same streets, shared similar trauma, or come from rival corners of the same community.

Motivational Interviewing is often taught as an individual method, but it also holds power in groups, if used with intention, skill, and cultural awareness.

This chapter explores how group dynamics affect engagement, how peer influence can serve as both a risk and a strength, and how MI can support transformation in the group setting, especially among African American participants.

Why Groups Can Be Triggering

Group spaces can feel threatening for Black clients, not because they're against community, but because they've had to protect themselves from community in some cases.

Some have been hurt or betrayed by people they trusted.

Others have reputations they feel they need to maintain.

Some were raised not to show emotion in front of other men.

Many are dealing with grief, violence, or trauma they've never named aloud.

In this setting, vulnerability can feel dangerous. And group facilitators who miss these dynamics risk reinforcing silence instead of creating space for truth.

MI in group settings asks us to meet that tension with curiosity, not control. It asks us to make space for slow trust, to celebrate even small shares, and to never shame someone for how they protect themselves.

When One Voice Takes Over

It's common in group work for one or two voices to dominate. In Black male groups, this may come from clients who are used to leading with bravado, control, or even humor. That voice might say:

"Man, this is all BS." "I've done this program ten times." "Y'all don't really want to stop."

It's easy to see these comments as disruptive, but often, they're a test: "Is this space strong enough to hold my truth?" If the group turns on them, they shut down. If the facilitator attacks, they push back. But if the facilitator reflects, validates, and redirects, that's when things can shift.

Try saying:

"Sounds like you've seen a lot of programs that didn't do much. You're not sure if this one's any different."

Or:

"You're challenging the group, maybe because you want it to be real, not just another fake conversation."

This re-centers the energy without shaming it. It also models a different way to speak hard truths.

Peer Influence: Threat or Opportunity?

In group, peers can be your biggest challenge or your most powerful tool. Some clients will come in with negative energy, testing boundaries or pulling others off track. But others will quietly lead just by how they show up.

That one client who says:

"I ain't perfect, but I'm here."

That's leadership.

That one who says:

"I used to think like that too, until I lost my cousin."

That's testimony.

The power of peer influence in Black communities is deep. Storytelling, street wisdom, and shared experience have always been vehicles of healing. MI encourages us to draw from that, not silence it.

Create moments where peer voices can echo MI values:

Invite group members to reflect back what they heard in someone's share.

Ask, "Has anyone else felt like that?"

When a client expresses change talk, ask, "What helped you get to that place?"

Let the group carry the weight of growth, not just the facilitator.

Handling Conflict and Keeping It Safe

Tension in group is normal. In fact, it often means people are starting to feel something. But safety must come first, especially in groups where trauma, pride, and street history are in the room.

Set clear norms early, and reinforce them with calm authority:

"We don't have to agree in here, but we do need to keep it respectful."

When conflict arises, use MI strategies to de-escalate:

"Sounds like something in that touched a nerve for you. Can we slow it down and check in?"

If things get heated, offer clients the option to take a break without punishment:

"It's okay to step out if this is too much. We can regroup when you're ready."

This shows that the space is strong enough to hold emotion, but also boundaried enough to protect everyone in it.

The Power of Shared Identity in Group

In Black-led groups or groups with facilitators of shared background, clients often say, "I can talk different in here." That's not just language—it's trust.

When clients see themselves reflected in leadership, they're more likely to drop the mask. They don't have to over-explain their pain. They don't have to defend their culture. They can just be.

MI techniques—reflections, affirmations, open-ended questions—take on even more power in that context, because they're not just therapeutic tools, they're acts of cultural alignment.

And even when the facilitator is not of the same background, a culturally humble approach acknowledging differences, listening deeply, honoring community wisdom can still create powerful connection.

Closing Reflection

Group work in Black communities is sacred work. It holds the possibility of healing that goes beyond any individual session. It can be a space where people remember they're not alone, where they hear their story in someone else's mouth, where shame breaks, where truth lands.

Motivational Interviewing in group doesn't mean managing behavior. It means nurturing collective courage. It means slowing down, holding space, and letting the room lead when it's ready.

Because sometimes the real breakthrough doesn't come from the counselor—it comes from the brother sitting next to you saying, "I've been there too."

Chapter 11

Spirituality, Legacy, and Healing Beyond the Session

Recovery in Black communities isn't just about getting clean it's about getting free. Free from addiction, yes. But also free from generational pain, invisible chains, and the silence that has lived in our families for too long.

And when you start talking about freedom in our communities, you can't separate that from spirituality.

Even when someone says, "I don't do church," or "I ain't religious," most still carry a spiritual framework. Whether it's rooted in the church, the ancestors, the streets, or the stars, Black people have always held on to something bigger than ourselves. That belief in something higher has carried us when nothing else could.

Motivational Interviewing, when practiced with cultural awareness, doesn't ignore this truth. It honors it. It listens for it. And it makes space for healing that stretches beyond behavior change—into the soul, into legacy, and into the future our people have been fighting to reach.

Spirituality is Already in the Room

You don't have to bring up God to be in a spiritual conversation. Sometimes clients will say:

"Somebody looking out for me.""It gotta be a reason I'm still here.""My grandma been gone, but I still hear her."

That's spiritual language.

That's a client reaching for meaning, for purpose, for something they can't always name but feel deep in their bones.

You don't need to label it. You just need to honor it.

"Sounds like you believe you've been protected through all of this.""Even in the middle of the chaos, there's a part of you that knows you're not alone."

You're not pushing belief—you're making space for it.

When Legacy Becomes a Reason to Change

For many Black clients, the turning point in recovery doesn't come from hitting rock bottom. It comes from realizing they want to leave something different behind.

"I don't want my kids to remember me like this."

"I'm trying to break the cycle."

"I've buried too many people, I can't go out like that."

This is legacy talk. This is someone thinking beyond the moment, beyond survival, beyond self.

MI helps people clarify what legacy means to them.

You can ask:

"What do you want to be remembered for?""What story do you want your family to tell about this part of your life?""When people say your name, what do you hope they feel?"

You're not asking for a perfect answer. You're inviting vision.

And when a Black man or woman reconnects with their own vision, their own purpose—that's where transformation gets rooted.

Honoring Ancestors, Naming Grief

Healing in Black communities is also about honoring those we've lost. Sometimes it's literal—mothers, brothers, cousins who died too soon. Sometimes it's emotional—the parts of ourselves we had to bury just to survive.

Grief is always in the room. And so are the ancestors.

"My pops did the same thing I'm doing now.""My uncle was the first one to shoot dope in front of me.""My sister got clean, but cancer took her."

These are not distractions. They're doorways.

You might say:

"Sounds like you're carrying them with you, even now.""What do you think they'd say if they could see you in this moment?""How do you want to honor them while you heal?"

This is not therapy jargon. This is sacred work. Because every person in recovery is not just healing themselves—they're healing backwards, through time, and forward, into generations they'll never meet.

When Faith Has Been Weaponized

For some clients, especially those hurt by religious institutions, the mention of God can bring up pain.

"I stopped believing a long time ago.""Church folk turned their back on me.""They told me I was going to hell."

We don't push past that. We sit in it.

"Sounds like faith used to be something that gave you comfort and now it's complicated.""You're holding a lot of pain from people who were supposed to care for you."

This opens space for spiritual redefinition. It says, "You don't have to throw it all away. You get to keep what still feeds you and let the rest go."

That's healing on a soul level.

Making Room for Ritual and Reflection

Many Black clients engage in practices that aren't labeled spiritual but are sacred all the same.

Lighting a candle for the dead

Playing gospel in the morning

Wearing grandma's old ring

Pouring out liquor for someone lost

Getting a tattoo to honor the fallen

These are rituals. Acts of remembrance. Small ceremonies that hold deep power.

In Motivational Interviewing, we can invite clients to name or reclaim these practices.

"Are there any traditions you hold that keep you grounded?""What helps you feel connected to something bigger when things get hard?""Is there a way you mark growth or milestones in your life?"

When you ask these questions, you're not just talking about coping—you're making space for soul work.

Closing Reflection

In Black communities, recovery is never just about stopping a substance. It's about reclaiming your name. Honoring who came before you. Healing so your children don't have to start from scratch. Rebuilding your connection to the divine, however you define it.

Motivational Interviewing must leave room for the spirit, the ancestors, the grief, and the glory.

Because in our culture, healing isn't just an individual act, it's a legacy move.

Chapter 12

Cultural Resistance to Treatment and the Power of Reframing

In the Black community, resistance to treatment is often misunderstood.

Professionals call it "noncompliance," "denial," or "ambivalence." But too often, what they label as resistance is actually protection. It's mistrust built from systems that harmed us. It's survival rooted in experience. It's wisdom that says, "Be careful who you open up to."

When we look at resistance through a cultural lens, we stop asking, "Why won't they engage?" and start asking, "What are they protecting themselves from?"

Motivational Interviewing, at its best, helps us see resistance not as a wall, but as a window. And with the right approach, we can meet that resistance with empathy, reframe it with respect, and use it as an opening for healing—not a barrier to it.

Resistance is a Form of Wisdom

Imagine being told to trust a system that jailed your cousin, overmedicated your uncle, and watched your mother suffer without help. Now imagine that same system offering you "treatment."

You'd be skeptical, too.

Resistance often sounds like:

"This program can't do nothing for me.""I'm only here so I don't go back to jail.""ain't nothing wrong with smoking a little weed.""These people don't know me."

Too many providers take that at face value. But beneath those words are deeper truths:

"I've never seen treatment work for someone like me."

"Opening up feels dangerous."

"I've learned not to show weakness."

"I've survived by keeping people out."

That's not defiance. That's wisdom.

MI teaches us to honor that wisdom—even if it looks like pushback.

Meeting Resistance with Reflection, Not Reaction

When clients resist, the natural urge is to correct, persuade, or defend the program. But that only deepens the divide.

Instead, MI teaches us to reflect the underneath of what's being said:

Client: "I don't need this group."Facilitator: "You're not sure if this group is really for you."

Client: "Y'all just here for a paycheck."Facilitator: "Feels like people in your life haven't always had your best interest in mind."

Client: "ain't no point in changing."Facilitator: "A part of you feels like change won't really change anything."

Each reflection is a door. It slows the moment down. It lets the client hear themselves without being judged. And often, that alone begins to shift the dynamic.

The Role of Pride and Image

For many Black men especially, resistance is tied to image. In a world where being vulnerable is seen as weak, many have learned to protect themselves with pride, silence, or even bravado.

"I've been through worse than this.""I don't need help. I just need time to get back on my feet.""This is just a phase. I'll bounce back."

These aren't lies. They're armor.

And the role of the MI practitioner isn't to strip that armor. It's to gently ask, "What's underneath it?"

Try:

"Sounds like you've always had to figure it out on your own.""You're used to being the one who holds it together.""You've learned to survive by not letting people see the struggle."

Affirm the strength and the cost. Because underneath the resistance is often exhaustion. Loneliness. The need for someone to say, "You don't have to carry all of this by yourself."

Reframing Treatment as Power, Not Punishment

Many Black clients come into treatment through court mandates, probation requirements, or crisis intervention. They're not walking in with curiosity—they're dragged in with conditions.

So naturally, they see treatment as punishment, not opportunity.

Motivational Interviewing helps us reframe that.

Client: "My PO made me come here. "Facilitator: "Sounds like this wasn't your choice—but maybe this space could still work for you."

Client: "ain't nothing wrong with smoking weed. "Facilitator: "You don't see it as a problem—but it's starting to create some consequences."

Client: "This is a waste of time. "Facilitator: "If you're going to be here anyway, maybe we can use the time in a way that actually benefits you."

The goal is not to convince—it's to plant a seed. And sometimes that seed doesn't sprout in session. But it's planted in the way someone was spoken to, in the dignity they were given, in the space they were offered to think out loud.

Allowing Cultural Expressions of Resistance

Some clients will challenge you with sarcasm, humor, or storytelling that seems to dodge the question.

That's not avoidance. That's cultural expression.

Humor is a shield, but also a connector.

Sarcasm is a test: "Can you hang with me?"

Storytelling isn't off-topic, it's how truth gets delivered.

Don't shut that down. Join it. Respect it. And then gently guide it.

"You've got a way of turning pain into humor. That takes skill.""Sounds like that story says a lot about what you've been through."

Then follow up with a curious question:

"What did that experience teach you about trusting people?""How did that shape the way you see help today?"

That's where the shift happens—from performing to processing.

Closing Reflection

Resistance is not the enemy of change. It's often the beginning of it.

In Black communities, what looks like pushback is often pain in disguise. What sounds like anger is often grief. What gets labeled "noncompliance" is sometimes just a cry for respect.

Motivational Interviewing, when done with cultural humility, meets resistance with reverence. It listens. It reflects. It honors. And eventually, it opens a space where people who said, "I don't need this," start saying, "Maybe I deserve more."

Because when you reframe treatment not as something done to you, but something you reclaim for yourself that's where the healing starts.

Chapter 13
Reentry, Restoration, and Reclaiming Identity

Reentry isn't just about getting out. It's about finding your way back to yourself after the system tried to erase you.

For many Black men and women, incarceration is more than time served—it's a tearing away. From family. From identity. From purpose. And when they walk back into the world, the welcome mat is often missing.

Doors are closed. Records follow. Trust is broken. And people expect you to "just get it together," like you weren't locked in a cage, fighting for dignity every day.

That's why reentry work must be restorative, not just logistical. It's not just about housing and jobs. It's about healing what was taken. Rebuilding what was lost. And helping people remember who they were before the charges, before the number, before the trauma.

Motivational Interviewing has a powerful role to play here. Not as a checklist, but as a bridge—back to self, back to hope, and back to a future that still belongs to them.

The First Lie: "You Paid Your Debt"

Society loves to say, "You did your time, now move on." But we know that's a lie.

The truth is, for most returning citizens—especially Black ones—the sentence never really ends.

You can't get a job because of your background check.

You can't get housing because of your record.

You can't see your kids unless you prove you're "stable."

So when someone walks into a program or a clinic post-release, they're not just carrying their own doubt. They're carrying society's rejection.

That's why the MI mindset matters so much here. Instead of treating them like a risk to manage, we treat them like a person rebuilding—on their terms.

"Sounds like you're dealing with a lot of systems that still don't see your growth. ""You're not just trying to stay out, you're trying to build a life."

That reflection alone can be life-changing.

Identity After Incarceration

One of the deepest wounds of incarceration is what it does to your sense of self.

Prison doesn't just strip your freedom, it strips your name. It reduces you to "inmate," "offender," "felon." And if you're not careful, you start believing those are the only titles that fit.

So, when you get out, it's not just about physical reentry. It's about identity restoration.

MI invites people to ask:

"Who were you before all this?""Who are you becoming now?""What parts of you do you want to reclaim?"

We don't rush people into positivity. We let them name the harm and then help them redefine the narrative.

Client: "I was nothing but a dope boy."Facilitator: "That's how you survived but it sounds like you've always had hustle, leadership, strategy. What could that look like now?"

We help them shift the lens—from what they did to what they can become.

The Role of Shame and Stigma

Shame is a silent killer in the reentry journey.

Shame about what you did.

Shame about who you hurt.

Shame about who you became to survive.

And in the Black community, where so many families have been impacted by incarceration, that shame often turns into silence. We don't talk about it. We don't process it. We just try to keep moving.

MI makes space for that silence to break.

"What have you been carrying since you got out?""Who do you still feel you need to make peace with?""What would it look like to forgive yourself?"

That last question stops people in their tracks. Because many were never told that forgiveness was even an option.

Navigating Old Environments

One of the hardest parts of reentry is going back to the same neighborhood, the same people, the same triggers—with a new mindset.

A client might say:

"I'm trying to stay clean, but everybody around me still using.""They don't believe I've changed.""It's like the streets calling me back."

This isn't weakness. This is real life.

And instead of judging that, MI meets it with strategy and compassion:

"You're in a place where you're changing—but your environment hasn't.""Sounds like you're trying to build a new chapter in the middle of an old book."

We explore options. We affirm the strength it takes to break cycles in the same space they started.

And when possible, we connect them to peer mentors, especially those who've been through reentry themselves. Because the words hit different when they come from someone who knows the terrain.

Lifting Up Strength and Legacy

We never reduce returning citizens to their lowest moments.

Instead, we lift up the resilience it took to survive, the courage it takes to change, and the legacy they're now writing.

A man who spent ten years inside and shows up for his son every day, that's restoration.A woman who relapsed but came back to group anyway, that's accountability.A brother who says, "I ain't who I used to be", that's growth.

MI helps them name it. Claim it. Build from it.

"What are you proud of in yourself today?""What would the old you say about the you sitting here right now?""What do you want to pass down that's different than what you received?"

That's the real work. Not just staying out of jail—but walking into freedom, fully.

Closing Reflection

Reentry is one of the most sacred parts of the recovery journey. Because it's where people reclaim what the system tried to steal: their identity, their voice, their future.

And Motivational Interviewing, when rooted in cultural truth, can be a tool of restoration. It helps people see themselves not just as survivors but as storytellers, leaders, and cycle breakers.

Because reentry isn't just about staying out, it's about coming back to yourself.

Chapter 14
Trauma, Truth-Telling, and Healing the Wounds We Don't Name

We don't always call it trauma.

In the Black community, we call it "what we went through," "what we don't talk about," or "just the way it is." We normalize pain so well, we forget it's pain. We survive so well, we forget survival isn't the same as healing.

But the truth is—a lot of our brothers and sisters are walking around wounded. Carrying childhood violence, community violence, racism, incarceration, betrayal, abandonment, grief—and never calling it by name.

Motivational Interviewing gives us a chance to open space for those truths. Not with pity. Not with pressure. But with presence.

Because healing don't start when the therapist starts talking—it starts when the person across from you feels safe enough to speak.

What Trauma Sounds Like in Session

Trauma doesn't always walk in the door screaming. Sometimes it shows up in silence. In anger. In jokes. In a shrug that says, "I don't talk about that."

A client might say:

"I don't trust nobody." "I've been on my own since I was thirteen." "That's just the way I was raised."

They're telling you something important but coded. Trauma is in the subtext. And your job as an MI practitioner is to listen between the lines.

You don't rush. You don't pry. You reflect gently:

"Sounds like you learned early not to depend on people. ""You've had to protect yourself for a long time.""That experience shaped the way you see the world."

That's how we start unpacking trauma—not by asking for details, but by naming the survival behind the behavior.

We've Been Told to Stay Silent

Let's be real, Black folks have been told for generations to suck it up.

"What happens in this house stays in this house."

"You better not cry."

"ain't nobody got time for therapy."

This silence was passed down like a survival tool. And in many ways, it worked. But now it's choking us. Holding our pain hostage. Making us explode or numb out because we were never taught how to name what hurts.

MI invites truth-telling in a way that respects that legacy but challenges the silence.

"Sounds like you've had to hold a lot in. ""What would it feel like to say it out loud?""You don't owe me your story but you deserve to speak your truth."

We don't push we invite. And that invitation can be a turning point.

Trauma is in the Body Too

A lot of our people walk into treatment thinking they're there for addiction but addiction is often just the surface. Underneath? Unhealed trauma living in the body.

Anxiety that never goes away.

Rage that comes out of nowhere.

Insomnia that's lasted for years.

Tension in the shoulders, the chest, the stomach.

MI helps us connect those dots, carefully.

"You mentioned you've been on edge for a long time—when did that start?""You said you don't feel safe even when nothing's happening. That sounds exhausting. ""What helps your body feel calm, even if just for a moment?"

These aren't clinical questions. These are human questions. Rooted in respect. Asked with care.

When Trauma Leads to Addiction

Sometimes a client will say:

"I just like to get high.""Weed helps me chill.""Drinking keeps me from flipping out."

It sounds like preference. But often, it's pain management.

So we explore:

"What do you notice about how you feel before you use?""What would you have to face if you didn't have that to numb the pain?""What's the hardest part about being sober, emotionally?"

We're not trying to strip their coping—we're trying to understand it. And once we do, we can work with it.

"So using helped you survive—but now it's starting to hurt you too."

That truth hits different when it's reflected without judgment.

Giving Permission to Grieve

One of the deepest, quietest traumas in our community is grief. And we rarely get time, space, or language to process it.

Losing a brother to gun violence.

Watching your mother fade from addiction.

Being locked up when your cousin died—and not getting to say goodbye.

Our people carry unprocessed grief like bricks in their chest. And sometimes, all they need is permission.

"You ever get the chance to really mourn that loss?""What do you carry from that loss today?""If you could speak to them now, what would you say?"

Even when tears don't come, the shift does. Because grief deserves witness. And healing deserves time.

Closing Reflection

Trauma is not weakness. It's the mark of survival.

And when Black folks show up in treatment with guardedness, anger, or silence—it's not resistance. It's history. It's pain that was never given a safe place to land.

Motivational Interviewing, when done with deep cultural humility, creates that place. It opens space for stories long buried. It honors the strength it took to survive. And it gently invites healing—not by force, but by relationship.

Because when we name our wounds, we stop bleeding in silence.And when we tell the truth—we start to live free.

Chapter 15
In the Black community, healing rarely happens alone

We've always been a people of the circle, whether it was a family gathered in the living room, a block party on the corner, or a prayer group in the basement. Our power lives in collective experience. And yet, when it comes to treatment, so many of the groups we walk into feel cold, clinical, disconnected from how we actually heal.

We sit in rows. We read handouts. We're told to "share when ready." But the rhythm is off. The soul is missing.

If we're going to bring real Motivational Interviewing into Black spaces, we have to reshape the group setting into what it was always meant to be a healing circle. A place where stories are honored, truth is spoken, and connection does the heavy lifting.

Because the opposite of addiction isn't just sobriety—it's belonging.

Why Traditional Groups Don't Always Work for Us

Let's be honest. Most traditional group therapy formats were not designed with our people in mind.

They're overly structured.

They expect emotional vulnerability with strangers.

They penalize silence or humor as avoidance.

They treat anger like a problem, not a symptom.

So we get brothers and sisters walking in, sitting with their arms folded, cracking jokes, or just flat-out not coming back.

But when you look closer, that's not apathy it's disconnection. It's walking into a space and feeling like it wasn't built for you.

Motivational Interviewing can change that, if we let the culture shape the room.

What a Healing Circle Looks Like

A healing circle isn't about perfection—it's about presence.

It's a space where people can bring their full selves. Where trauma isn't rushed. Where silence is respected. Where pain and laughter can live in the same hour.

Picture it:

Chairs in a circle, not a line.

Music playing softly before the group starts, maybe gospel, soul, or lo-fi jazz.

Candles lit. Or incense. Or just the lights dimmed to soften the edge of the day.

Someone opens with a reflection or quote from a Black author, elder, or ancestor.

It doesn't have to be therapy with a capital T. It has to be real.

Because once people feel safe, they stop performing. They start healing.

Using MI in the Group Setting

MI isn't just for one-on-one work. It thrives in groups—especially when the facilitator knows how to guide the energy without dominating the space.

Instead of lecturing, you invite.

"Let's check in—what's been weighing on y'all this week?""Anyone want to speak to how they handled stress without using?""What's one thing you're proud of—even if nobody else sees it?"

You reflect what's said, but you also reflect the emotion beneath it.

"Sounds like that took a lot of strength.""You're carrying guilt, but also growth.""You showed up here even when everything in you wanted to quit. That matters."

You model empathy. You show what it looks like to hold space. And slowly, others start to do the same for each other.

That's when a group becomes a community.

When Group Dynamics Get Messy

Let's be clear—group work is not always smooth.

People interrupt.

Old beefs surface.

Someone gets triggered and shuts down.

A client storms out.

That's real. And instead of controlling it, MI teaches us to respond with curiosity and calm.

"Seems like that struck a nerve—want to say more?""I'm noticing some tension in the room—how are we all feeling right now?""Let's pause—this space is for honesty, but also for respect."

And if someone gets loud or says something hard?

You don't shut them down—you guide them back.

"You're passionate about that—and that tells me it matters to you.""Sounds like there's a story behind that reaction. You're not alone in feeling it."

This is how we keep the circle sacred—even when it gets messy.

Cultural Wisdom in Group Spaces

In Black spaces, healing often comes through testimony.

Not a lecture. Not a worksheet. But a story. A moment. A breakthrough shared out loud.

"I used to be right where you are.""Let me tell you how I got through.""If I can change, you can too."

These moments don't need a clinical term. They need respect.

Let the group reflect back:

"I felt that.""I needed to hear that today.""That gave me hope."

That's MI in action—not just from the facilitator, but from the group itself.

And when a group starts doing that? You've built a circle. You've sparked transformation.

Closing Reflection

Group work in the Black community must look and feel different because our pain, our rhythm, our joy, and our healing are different.

Motivational Interviewing gives us the foundation. But culture gives it life.

So we build spaces that reflect us. We honor stories over stats. We let silence speak. We let laughter heal. And we never forget: we heal better together.

Because in the Black tradition, a circle isn't just a shape. It's a promise, that no one walks this road alone.

Chapter 16
Peer Support and Mentorship in MI

You can't heal in isolation—not from trauma, not from addiction, not from generational pain. That's why peer support is more than a strategy in our communities—it's a survival tool.

In the Black community, mentorship is sacred. Whether it was your uncle, your cousin, an older brother, or someone from the block who pulled you to the side and said, "You better than this," that moment mattered. It didn't need a degree. It needed love, respect, and lived experience.

When Motivational Interviewing is used by peers—those who've walked the walk, it hits different. The conversation changes. The walls come down. Because now it's not just "you need to change." It's, "I've been there. Let's talk."

Why Peer Support Works

Peer support is powerful because it's relational, not hierarchical. There's no clinical gap. No office door. Just presence. Just truth.

Black clients often show up guarded, rightfully so. But when the person across from them says:

"I know what it's like to wake up and not want to be here." "I used to use to numb the pain, too." "I came through it. And you can too."

That lands. That resonates. That heals.

Peer support changes recovery from a program to a community. It replaces shame with belonging. It replaces judgment with testimony.

Using MI as a Peer Mentor

MI isn't just for therapists. It belongs to anyone who holds space for change. That includes peer specialists, recovery coaches, group leaders, and street outreach workers.

But here's what makes MI powerful in the hands of a peer:

You don't come in as the expert.

You come in as the witness.

You reflect, not direct.

You ask, not assume.

Instead of saying, "You need to go to treatment," a peer trained in MI might say:

"What would getting clean mean for you right now?""Sounds like part of you wants something different.""What would have to shift for you to feel ready?"

That's the heart of it. Not pushing. Not fixing. But walking beside someone until their own motivation rises up.

Lived Experience is Clinical Gold

Too many systems treat peer support as an afterthought. They offer minimum training. Minimum pay. And no real seat at the table.

But here's the truth: lived experience is a form of expertise.

When someone says, "I know what withdrawal feels like," that's not a footnote. That's clinical gold.

When someone says, "Here's how I handled that same trigger," that's treatment in real time.

We need to stop treating peers like assistants and start treating them like essential guides.

When MI is rooted in lived experience, it becomes movement, not just method.

Boundaries and Burnout

Peer mentors often carry a heavy load. They hold the pain of others while still healing their own. That's sacred—but dangerous without support.

MI teaches empathy with boundaries.

You are present, but not consumed.

You reflect, but don't absorb.

You show up, but you also rest.

Peers need spaces to process their own emotions too. Because you can't pour from an empty cup. And in this work, too many brothers and sisters are burning out in silence.

We must protect peer support—not just praise it.

"You don't have to save everyone. Showing up fully is already sacred work." "Take time to refuel. Your story still matters, even when you're off the clock."

Peer-Led Healing Circles

Some of the most transformative healing spaces are not led by licensed therapists. They're led by people in recovery. In reentry. In community.

Peer-led healing circles, when infused with MI, can look like:

Open dialogue without pressure.

Sharing stories, not solutions.

Reflecting what's heard, not what's expected.

Honoring both the pain and the progress.

And when the facilitator says,

"I'm not here to judge you. I'm just here to walk with you,"

that's when the group exhales. That's when healing begins.

Closing Reflection

Peer support is not an accessory to recovery, it's a pillar. It reminds us that healing doesn't come from perfection, but from presence. From people who've been through the storm and are still standing.

When you combine MI with lived experience, you build a pathway that's real, relatable, and rooted in love.

Because sometimes, the most powerful words a person can hear are not, "I can fix you, " but,

"I see you. I've been there. And you're not alone."

Chapter 17
Black Men and Vulnerability in the Recovery Space

If you want to see the bravest man in the room, look for the one who tells the truth about his pain.

But Black men in America? We've been taught that vulnerability is weakness. That emotion is a liability. That silence is survival.

From the playground to prison yards, from locker rooms to living rooms—we were told:

"Man up." "Don't cry." "You soft." "Handle it."

So we stuffed it down. All of it. The grief. The fear. The trauma. The confusion. The shame. And we wore masks that made us look strong but kept us from healing.

Motivational Interviewing gives us a chance to crack those masks. To honor what we've carried. To say to a Black man—not "be strong," but "you're safe here."

This chapter isn't about changing Black men. It's about giving them permission to be whole.

The Mask We Learn to Wear

The average Black man walks into treatment with decades of armor.

Stoicism that looks like apathy.

Humor that hides the hurt.

Rage that protects the wound.

Silence that speaks louder than words.

This isn't resistance. It's protection.

When a brother says:

"I ain't got nothin' to say." "I don't trust none of y'all." "I just came to get my paper signed."

What he's really saying might be:

"I've never been safe enough to open up." "I'm tired of being judged." "I don't know how to talk about this."

Motivational Interviewing doesn't push through that wall—it sits with it. It respects the armor, even as it gently asks:

"What's been the hardest part about carrying all this alone?" "If you didn't have to prove anything today, what would you want to say?" "What does strength mean to you—right now?"

That's where the door opens. That's where vulnerability can enter.

Vulnerability is a Rebellion

In a country that criminalizes, stereotypes, and dehumanizes Black men, being emotionally honest is revolutionary.

To say:

"I'm scared I'll mess up again."

"I feel like a failure."

"I don't know who I am without the hustle."

That takes more courage than any street fight ever did.

And when a practitioner—especially one outside the culture—hears that, the response matters.

You don't analyze it. You don't rush it.You say:

"Thank you for trusting me with that." "That's real." "You're not alone in feeling that."

You hold it. You honor it. And you let that moment land.

Because for many Black men, that is the turning point. Not the treatment plan. Not the urine test. But being seen without being reduced.

When Vulnerability Feels Unsafe

Some brothers will tell you straight up:

"Where I come from, being open gets you killed." "I've been played every time I let my guard down." "Therapy ain't for dudes like me."

They're not lying. Vulnerability has been weaponized against us. In families. In relationships. In courtrooms. Even in recovery.

So we don't push vulnerability—we make it safe.

That means:

Respecting silence.

Not rushing emotion.

Asking permission before going deep.

Creating space for emotional literacy, one word at a time.

You might say:

"Sounds like letting people in has come with pain." "If you choose to share, I'll listen without judgment." "You don't have to go there today—but if and when you do, I'll be here."

That's not therapy talk. That's trauma-informed, culturally grounded presence.

When Other Black Men Hold Space

There's a unique power in Black men being vulnerable with each other.

When one brother speaks up:

"I ain't been okay since my brother died." "I'm trying to be a father, but I never had one." "I used to numb everything with pills because I didn't want to feel."

And another says:

"I feel that." "Me too." "I got you."

That's when shame dissolves. That's when isolation breaks. That's when healing becomes collective.

We need more circles where Black men can speak and not be silenced. Cry and not be ridiculed. Reflect and not be feared.

Because we heal better when we heal together.

Redefining What It Means to Be a Man

MI helps Black men reflect on the roles they've been forced to play. It gives them space to ask:

"What kind of man do I actually want to be?" "Who told me I had to be hard all the time?" "What does strength look like now that I'm trying to heal?"

And we affirm:

"Vulnerability is not weakness, it's truth." "You don't have to earn your worth—it's already yours." "Being a man doesn't mean you carry it alone."

This is more than treatment. This is identity work. This is liberation.

Closing Reflection

To sit with a Black man in recovery and hear him say,

"I don't have to pretend anymore,"is holy.

To see him cry and not apologize is sacred.

To watch him show up for himself, raw and real, is a miracle of resistance.

Motivational Interviewing, when grounded in cultural humility, becomes a tool for truth-telling, not just behavior change.

Because when a Black man becomes vulnerable, he's not breaking down, he's breaking through.

Chapter 18

Addressing Systemic Racism in the Therapeutic Relationship

You can't separate the therapeutic relationship from the system it lives in.

We don't meet clients in a vacuum—we meet them in a world that has failed them, criminalized them, dismissed them, and written them off.

So if we want to use Motivational Interviewing with integrity in Black communities, we have to be willing to name what's real:

Systemic racism isn't just outside the clinic—it walks into the room with the client.

If you ignore that truth, you become part of the harm.

This chapter is about how we hold space for recovery while holding truth about the systems that surround us. Because healing doesn't happen when we avoid discomfort. It happens when we face it, together.

When the System Has Already Spoken

Many Black clients walk into treatment having been told, explicitly or implicitly:

You're a risk, not a person.

You're a case file, not a father.

You're a number, not a name.

They've been arrested, suspended, labeled, surveilled, misdiagnosed, under-resourced, and over-policed.

So when they sit down in front of a provider, especially a white one, the question isn't "Are you qualified?" It's, "Can I trust you not to hurt me like they did?"

If you don't name that unspoken truth, the client will hold it alone and the room will never feel safe.

You don't have to have the same experience. But you do have to be willing to say:

"I know that people who look like me have often harmed people who look like you in these systems.""If any part of this feels like another system trying to control you, I want us to talk about that."

This isn't political—it's personal. It's relational accountability.

Cultural Mistrust Isn't Resistance. It's Survival.

When a Black client doesn't open up, it's not always "resistance to treatment."Sometimes, it's a trauma response to a lifetime of being unheard, misread, and punished.

You might hear:

"I don't mess with these programs.""Y'all just trying to get me to say something I'll regret.""It don't matter what I say—it's already written."

This isn't oppositional behavior—it's informed caution.

MI helps us slow down and reflect:

"Sounds like you've had experiences where your voice didn't matter.""You're used to people assuming the worst—and that's real.""You're not wrong for being cautious. And I'm here to earn your trust, not demand it."

In that moment, you're not just using a technique—you're undoing some of the weight of history.

Practicing Cultural Humility, Not Cultural Competence

There is no checklist for understanding a Black client. No training that gives you a pass.

Instead, we ask:

"Am I willing to be uncomfortable?""Am I listening more than I'm speaking?""Am I checking my own bias when it shows up?"

Cultural humility means:

Being open to correction.

Welcoming feedback without defensiveness.

Naming your own positionality, especially when power is imbalanced.

MI aligns perfectly here—it invites us to lead with curiosity, empathy, and transparency.

"I don't know what it's like to live your story—but I want to understand it better.""If anything I say ever lands wrong, I hope you'll tell me. You deserve that space."

That's how you stop being another part of the system—and start becoming a part of the healing.

When Systems Create Barriers to Change

Sometimes the client is ready to grow—but the system isn't ready to support them.

They want to stay clean, but can't find housing.

They want to reunite with their kids, but CPS keeps moving the goalpost.

They want a job, but their record follows them everywhere.

In these moments, MI allows us to hold both:

"You've done your part but the system isn't showing up for you.""It's okay to feel tired. None of this has been fair.""What do you need right now—to survive this moment, and to keep moving forward?"

This is where advocacy and empathy meet. You validate the injustice without ever letting the client's fire go out.

When the Practitioner Is Black

Even when the provider is also Black, the system is still in the room.

Black clinicians are often expected to bridge cultural understanding, absorb generational pain, and translate institutional trauma—all while managing their own.

To Black providers reading this:

You're not just clinicians. You're culture holders.You're not just helpers. You're witnes ses.And you don't owe anyone perfection to be powerful in this work.

MI is a tool that can help you protect your energy while still honoring your commun ity.Use it to uplift, not overextend.

"I'm here with you—not above you.""We've both had to navigate systems that weren't built for us.""Let's talk about what healing looks like—for you."

That's what it means to hold the line. That's what it means to heal while you help.

Closing Reflection

Systemic racism shapes the context in which we do this work—but it does not get the final word.

Motivational Interviewing becomes transformative when it makes space for that truth. When it tells a Black client,

"You are not crazy. You are not broken. The system is not neutral and you deserve more.
"

That's not political. That's ethical. That's clinical. That's human.

Because until the system is just, the most radical thing we can do is create one small space where a Black person feels seen, heard, and respected, without condition.

Chapter 19

The Role of the Practitioner—Cultural Humility Over Cultural Competence

Let's be clear: you will never "master" someone else's culture.

You can't attend a few trainings, learn the slang, memorize the holidays, and call yourself culturally competent. Culture is not a checklist. It's a lived experience—fluid, complex, and shaped by history, geography, language, trauma, pride, and resistance.

So let's retire the myth of cultural competence and replace it with something deeper, more honest, and more human:

Cultural humility.

This chapter is about what it means to show up, not as an expert, not as a fixer, but as a partner in healing. It's a call to practitioners to do their own work, confront their own bias, and approach every conversation with a willingness to listen, learn, and grow.

Because in Motivational Interviewing, the practitioner's spirit matters just as much as the method.

Competence Assumes Mastery. Humility Honors Humanity.

The term "competence" can imply arrival. Like you've arrived at understanding another culture. But humility says:

"I'm always learning." "I don't know what I don't know." "You are the expert on your own story."

Cultural humility is a posture, not a credential. It means acknowledging that:

You carry bias, even if you don't intend to.

Power dynamics are always present.

You are capable of harm, even when your goal is to help.

That's not shame—it's accountability.

And MI gives us the tools to lean into that accountability without losing connection. Instead of defending yourself, you reflect:

"Sounds like something I said didn't land the way I meant it. Can you help me understand that better?""I appreciate you trusting me enough to name that—I want to make sure I do better.""I know I have blind spots. Please let me know if something I do feels off."

That's how trust is built. Not by perfection, but by presence.

The MI Practitioner as a Mirror, Not a Mold

Too often, practitioners—especially those trained in traditional Western clinical models—come in ready to fix. Ready to correct, diagnose, and prescribe change.

But MI doesn't ask us to shape the client—it asks us to reflect them back to themselves.

That's a sacred task.

It means:

Listening without control.

Asking without agenda.

Affirming without condescension.

You don't say, "You need to stop smoking."You say, "What does smoking do for you right now—and what's it costing you?"You don't say, "You're in denial."You say, "Sounds like part of you sees a problem—and part of you is still weighing it."

In Black communities, where help has often come with harm, this approach changes everything. It tells the client: "You lead. I walk with you."

That's humility in action.

Confronting Internal Bias and Power

No matter how good your intentions are, you bring your own worldview into the room. Your own judgments. Your own assumptions. Your own fears.

Cultural humility means naming that:

"I notice I have more resistance when the client is loud—where did I learn that?""Am I interpreting this behavior through a white, middle-class lens?""Am I responding to this brother as a client—or as a stereotype I've been conditioned to fear?"

This is the work behind the work.

And it's not just for white providers. Black clinicians, too, have to unlearn respectability politics, anti-Blackness, and professional roles that reward disconnection.

We ask:

"Am I creating safety—or just performing it?""Am I holding space or managing behavior?""Am I seeing the person or the paperwork?"

This isn't about shame, it's about liberation. Because when you free yourself from the need to be the expert, you make room for something real to emerge.

Practicing Radical Empathy Without Saviorism

Empathy doesn't mean pity. And humility doesn't mean silence. In this work, practitioners must learn the difference between solidarity and saviorism.

Saviorism says:

"Let me rescue you."

"I know what's best."

"You wouldn't make it without me."

Solidarity says:

"I see your strength, even in your struggle."

"I will walk with you, not in front of you."

"I trust your capacity to lead your own healing."

MI teaches us to be guides—not gatekeepers. To help clients hear their own voice—not replace it with ours.

That's especially important when working across racial, cultural, or economic lines. Humility keeps us from slipping into hero mode. And it keeps the focus where it belongs—on the client's truth.

The Ongoing Practice of Reflection

Cultural humility is not a one-time realization, it's a daily practice.

It looks like:

Regular supervision that includes cultural exploration.

Seeking feedback from clients about your impact.

Engaging in therapy or peer reflection for your own growth.

Reading, listening, and learning from voices outside your experience.

It also means being okay with discomfort. Growth is uncomfortable. But it's also sacred.

"You don't have to be perfect to be powerful. You just have to be present, honest, and willing to grow."

That's the kind of practitioner this manual calls for.

Closing Reflection

The most effective MI practitioner isn't the one who has all the answers. It's the one who can sit with the question, hold space for the tension, and still lead with love.

Cultural humility invites you to show up fully human—in service of another human.

Not above. Not ahead. But beside.

Because at the end of the day, this work is not about fixing people—it's about helping them remember who they are, what they carry, and what's possible on the other side of pain.

Chapter 20

Bringing It All Together—Practice, Policy, and Power

This manual is more than pages of guidance. It's a declaration: We deserve treatment that reflects our humanity, our history, and our healing. Black people deserve therapeutic spaces that see us fully—without judgment, assumption, or erasure.

Motivational Interviewing, when done with cultural humility and deep respect, has the power to transform not just individuals, but entire systems.

But to do that, we must move from theory to practice, from the individual to policy, and from empathy to power.

Practice: Walking the Talk

If you're holding this manual, you're likely in the work—maybe as a counselor, a peer, a case manager, a group facilitator, or a leader. Regardless of your title, here's what real practice looks like:

You build rapport without rushing.

You reflect without controlling.

You affirm without performative praise.

You ask, "What do you want for yourself?" not "What's wrong with you?"

Real practice sounds like:

"You've survived a lot. What's kept you going?""You say part of you wants to change, and part of you's unsure. That makes sense.""How do you define success, for you, not for them?"

Every interaction is a chance to restore dignity. Every session is a chance to return voice. Every client is a mirror of someone's brother, uncle, father, son—or self.

The healing is in the relationship. And relationships built on respect, truth, and cultural awareness save lives.

Policy: Changing the Rules of Engagement

You can be the most culturally grounded practitioner in the world, but if the policies surrounding you are rooted in oppression, your work is being undermined.

So we don't just stop at client care. We push systems to evolve.

That means advocating for:

Funding for peer-led, culturally rooted programs.

Ending criminalization of substance use and mental illness.

Hiring and retaining Black practitioners—not as tokens, but as leaders.

Policies that don't just measure outcomes, but honor process.

It also means rejecting one-size-fits-all approaches. Black clients don't need to be forced into white, middle-class models of healing. They need support rooted in their values, their language, their pace.

We fight for systems that see culture not as a barrier—but as a bridge.

Power: Who Gets to Define Recovery?

Recovery is more than sobriety. For Black people, recovery also means recovering from:

Generational trauma

Mass incarceration

Forced displacement

Educational harm

Economic disenfranchisement

Medical mistrust

Spiritual disconnection

We are not just recovering from drugs or alcohol—we are recovering from the conditions that created the need to numb ourselves in the first place.

That's why the definition of recovery must be owned by the people living it.

True power is giving the pen back to the people who've had their stories written for them.

And when Motivational Interviewing is practiced through that lens? It stops being a technique and becomes a movement.

A movement for:

Centering Black voices in behavioral health.

Training Black facilitators and authors.

Supporting Black-led healing spaces.

Shifting from compliance to connection.

Moving from passive service delivery to community-led liberation.

This Manual Is a Tool—But You Are the Strategy

This manual can't do the work for you. It can't build the trust, hold the silence, or reflect the pain.

You do that.

But with this manual, you don't have to do it alone. You now hold a culturally adapted guide rooted in lived experience, professional practice, and love for Black people.

You hold something that says, "We're not invisible. We're not resistant. We're not broken. We are brilliant. We are ready. And we are rising."

Final Words

To the Black man walking into treatment for the first time, unsure if anyone will ever understand him: We see you.

To the practitioner trying to do right by your clients while navigating unjust systems: Keep going. You matter.

To the people who've been harmed by the very places meant to help them: You deserve better. This is one step toward that.

Let this manual be a door—not a gate.

Let it be a guide—not a gospel.

And let it be a start—not the end.

We are not just adapting Motivational Interviewing for African Americans, we are reclaiming the power to heal in our own image.

Chapter 21

Final Notes

Final Notes

This manual is not the finish line. It is the beginning of a new way of seeing, engaging, and walking with Black clients through recovery.

Print it. Share it. Teach from it. Challenge it. And above all—live it.

If this manual changed the way you show up for your clients, let it also change the way you show up for yourself.

Because healing, when rooted in truth and dignity, is contagious.

And Black healing is not just possible, it's already happening.

Chapter 22

Acknowledgments II

Thank You

First and foremost, I give thanks to the men who've sat across from me, numb, raw, guarded, grieving, and still showing up. Your courage, even when unspoken, has been the heartbeat of this work. This manual was written with you in mind.

To every Black man who has been told he was too angry, too broken, too difficult, or too far gone, know that your healing matters. Your story matters. You matter.

To the practitioners who truly listen, who challenge systems, who don't shrink from uncomfortable truths, thank you. You are not just delivering treatment—you are changing lives and protecting dignity.

To my colleagues, peers, and mentors who have walked with me on this path of recovery, justice, and leadership, your wisdom helped shape this work.

To those who shared feedback, lifted up my voice, and encouraged me to write this manual in the fullness of who I am, thank you for honoring not just my ideas, but my experience.

And to the next generation of Black leaders in behavioral health: take this, improve it, expand it. The work is yours now.

Chapter 23
References

Miller, W. R., & Rollnick, S. (2013). Motivational Interviewing: Helping People Change (3rd ed.). New York: Guilford Press.

Sue, D. W., & Sue, D. (2015). Counseling the Culturally Diverse: Theory and Practice (7th ed.). Wiley.

Substance Abuse and Mental Health Services Administration (SAMHSA). (2019). TIP 35: Enhancing Motivation for Change in Substance Use Disorder Treatment.

Garrett, M. T., & Herring, R. D. (2001). Honoring the Power of the Circle: Motivational Interviewing with Native American People.

Harris, M. , & Fallot, R. (2001). Using Trauma Theory to Design Service Systems. Jossey-Bass.

hooks, bell. (2004). The Will to Change: Men, Masculinity, and Love. Washington Square Press.

West, C. (1993). Race Matters. Beacon Press.

Holley, L. C., & Steiner, S. (2005). Safe spaces: Creating culturally responsive environments for African American clients. Families in Society.

Ginlack, K. (2025). Motivational Interviewing for African Americans: A Culturally Grounded Guide.

Chapter 24

Appendix A:

Sample Affirmations Adapted for African American Clients

Affirmations are a core tool in Motivational Interviewing, meant to build self-efficacy, validate strengths, and reinforce a client's ability to move toward change. But for African American clients, affirmations need to go deeper than surface-level praise. They must recognize the resilience shaped by history, the strength required to survive racism, and the dignity of simply showing up.

Below are sample affirmations that reflect that cultural context.

Affirmations Rooted in Cultural Truth

"You've carried a lot and you're still standing—that's strength."

"What you're doing right now, even just being here, is an act of resistance."

"You weren't supposed to make it this far—and yet, here you are."

"I can hear how much you care, even in your anger. That's real."

"You've been navigating a world that hasn't always seen your worth. That takes wisdom."

"It sounds like you've made a lot of sacrifices to protect your people. That says a lot about your character."

"You found a way to survive when you didn't have many options. That's resourcefulness."

"You know how to lead, even if you haven't always had the title."

"There's a fire in you. That fire has kept you alive."

"You've had every reason to give up, but you haven't. That's power."

Group-Based Affirmations for Peer Recovery Circles

"You don't have to be perfect to be powerful. Your voice matters in this space."

"There's nothing weak about healing. That's where your power begins."

"Every time you show up, you show others what's possible."

"You're not alone—we walk this together."

"I see your growth even if you don't see it yet."

Why These Matter

For some clients, these affirmations might be the first time they've heard something affirming without it being tied to performance, behavior, or compliance. Affirmations that honor who they are, not just what they've done, build trust and disrupt internalized messages of inferiority.

They also reflect the reality that healing in the Black community is not just about the individual—it's about reclaiming power, dignity, and legacy.

Chapter 25

Appendix B:

Sample Reflections Reworded for Cultural Responsiveness

Reflections are a cornerstone of Motivational Interviewing—they show that we're listening, that we understand, and that we're walking with the client, not just watching them from a distance.

But for African American clients, especially those who have been historically talked down to or misunderstood, reflections need to feel authentic, human, and real. They should invite openness, not trigger defensiveness. The tone matters. The words matter.

Below are examples of culturally grounded reflections, phrased in ways that preserve the MI spirit, while honoring the lived realities of Black clients.

Common Clinical Reflections (and Culturally Adapted Versions)

Use everyday language.

Clinical jargon can feel like a barrier.

Honor the struggle. Don't minimize what they've been through.

Validate both sides. Reflect ambivalence without judgment.

Listen for what's unsaid. Silence and body language carry weight.

Use tone intentionally. The way you reflect matters as much as the words.

Closing Thought

Reflections should sound like someone who's been in the room before. Someone who knows what it's like to have trust broken, dignity questioned, and options taken away. When you reflect that reality with care, clients don't just feel heard—they feel safe.

Chapter 26

Appendix C:

Open-ended questions are foundational in Motivational Interviewing

They create space for clients to express their values, motivations, and conflicts in their own words. But for African American clients—especially those who have experienced judgment, surveillance, or dehumanization from authority figures—questions must feel safe, non-intrusive, and genuinely curious, not clinical or interrogative.

The goal is not to gather data. The goal is to build connection.

Below are sample open-ended questions that reflect the lived experience, language, and trust-building needed when working with Black clients in recovery and change processes.

Building Trust and Engagement

"What was going through your mind when you first walked in here?"

"What made you decide to come today—even if you didn't want to?"

"What do you think people don't understand about your story?"

"How have you been surviving up to this point?"

"What do you want me to know about you before we even get started?"

Exploring Ambivalence and Motivation

"What's pulling you toward change—and what's holding you back?"

"When you picture the life you want, what's in it?"

"What part of you wants to keep doing things the same—and why?"

"What would 'better' look like for you—not anybody else?"

"What would make this process actually worth it to you?"

Unpacking Cultural and Systemic Experiences

"Have you felt judged or misunderstood by people trying to help you before?"

"What role has race played in how you've been treated by the system?"

"How have you had to protect yourself emotionally, just to get by?"

"What's it like being a Black man (or woman) trying to heal in this world?"

"How do you usually deal with pain when you can't talk to anyone?"

Inviting Personal Power and Agency

"If you had the tools and the support, what would you change first?"

"What would it look like for you to be in control—not the system, not the substance?"

"Who believes in you, even when you don't believe in yourself?"

"What strengths do you have that people overlook?"

"What are you proud of, even if nobody's said it out loud?"

Why These Questions Matter

For many Black clients, being asked the right question at the right time—without judgment, without pressure—is an act of liberation. These questions don't demand. They invite. They tell the client: "Your voice matters. Your experience matters. And we are not here to fix you. We're here to walk with you."

Chapter 27

Appendix D:

Group Guidelines for Culturally Grounded MI Sessions

Group settings offer a space for collective healing, shared wisdom, and relational accountability. But for African American clients, groups can also bring layers of vulnerability, mistrust, and survival-driven silence—especially if past group experiences felt judgmental, disorganized, or irrelevant to their lived experience.

Culturally grounded group facilitation requires intentional structure that promotes dignity, voice, and belonging—not just behavior management.

Below are guidelines to support group spaces rooted in safety, power-sharing, and cultural resonance.

Foundational Group Agreements

These can be co-created with participants, but facilitators should ensure they're upheld consistently:

What's said here stays here.Confidentiality is real. Gossip or street talk outside the group breaks trust.

We don't shame anyone's process.Everyone moves at their own pace. No one gets mocked, rushed, or dismissed.

We let each other finish. Interrupting is not just rude, it silences survival stories. Let people speak their full truth.

We speak from "I" statements.No lectures. No fixing. Just your truth.

You don't have to talk, but we invite you in.Silence is respected. Participation is never forced—but your voice is welcomed.

We hold space, not power.No one dominates. No one gets ignored.

We acknowledge the outside world is real. What we talk about here—racism, family, court, trauma—isn't "off-topic." It's part of the healing.

Facilitator Practices

To honor the spirit of Motivational Interviewing and Black cultural strength, facilitators should:

Model vulnerability. Let clients see your humanity. That doesn't weaken your leadership, it strengthens it.

Redirect without shaming. If a group member goes off-topic or becomes disruptive, respond with curiosity, not control.

Bring in music, stories, and art. Culture heals. Spoken word, gospel, hip hop, or ancestral proverbs can deepen meaning more than a worksheet ever could.

Know your own biases. Check yourself constantly. Your tone, reactions, and silence all speak.

Uplift leadership in the room. Let the men and women in the group lead conversations, suggest topics, or pose questions. That's how trust grows.

Sample Group Check-In Questions

Start each group with one of these to build rapport and shared presence:

"What did you have to push through just to make it here today?"

"What's been heavy on your mind that you haven't said out loud?"

"What does strength look like for you this week?"

"What's something you wish more people understood about your struggle?"

Closing Rounds

Never end group cold. Leave space for closure, affirmation, and choice.

"One word to describe how you're leaving today?"

"Something you heard that stuck with you?"

"What are you taking with you—and what are you leaving behind?"

Final Thought

Groups work best when they stop feeling like therapy and start feeling like family—real, honest, sometimes messy, but grounded in mutual respect and a shared desire to get free.

Chapter 28

Appendix E:

Addressing Common Client Statements with Cultural Sensitivity

Motivational Interviewing is all about engaging the client where they are, without judgment, without force, and without assumptions. But when working with African American clients, some statements carry deeper weight. They may reflect not just personal resistance, but cultural protection, historical mistrust, or trauma-based responses.

Below are real-world statements often heard in practice, alongside suggested responses that reflect empathy, cultural awareness, and the MI spirit.

1. **"My PO made me come here. ain't nothing wrong with smoking weed."**

Culturally attuned response:"You didn't come here by choice, and I can respect that. Weed's been something that helps you deal with things. So let's start there. What does it do for you? What does it cost you?"

Why it matters:Instead of arguing about legality or consequences, we acknowledge the client's autonomy, honor their coping method, and start where they are.

2. **"You don't know what it's like out there. Talking ain't gonna change nothing."**

Response:"You're right—I haven't walked in your shoes. And I'm not here to fix you with words. I'm here to walk with you if you're open to that."

Why it matters:Acknowledging lived experience is key. Clients aren't looking to be impressed—they're watching for signs of respect.

3. **"Man, I've done this program before. It's the same bullshit."**

Response:"Sounds like you've seen the cycle—and you're tired of it. What would actually make this different for you?"

Why it matters:Rather than defend the program, we invite collaboration and restore power.

4. **"White people always think they know what's best for Black people."**

Response:"You're naming something real—and you have every right to feel that way. What's helped you tell the difference between people who see you, and people who don't?"

Why it matters:This isn't just frustration—it's a trauma-informed observation. Validate it. Stay present.

5. **"My cousin just got shot. So fuck this group right now."**

Response:"You're hurting and you're still here. That tells me something. You don't have to talk about it if you're not ready. But I see you."

Why it matters:Trauma shows up in the room whether we address it or not. This response affirms the pain and the power in their presence.

6. **"I ain't soft. I ain't tryna cry in front of y'all."**

Response:"Where we come from, showing emotion gets labeled as weak but what if it's actually one of the realest things you can do?"

Why it matters:This response reframes vulnerability as strength, not shame.

7. **"I don't trust nobody in here."**

Response:"You've got good reason to protect yourself. What would have to happen for this space to feel different for you?"

Why it matters:This honors survival instincts, rather than treating distrust as defiance.

Closing Note:

These aren't scripts, they're starting points. What matters most is how you show up, not just what you say. Cultural responsiveness lives in your tone, your timing, and your truth.

Chapter 29

Appendix F:

Practitioner Reflection Prompts for Cultural Self-Awareness

Motivational Interviewing requires more than technique, it demands presence, humility, and deep reflection. For practitioners working with African American clients, cultural self-awareness isn't optional. It's a responsibility.

This appendix offers prompts to help you check your own biases, unpack your cultural lens, and align your practice with the principles of justice and respect.

These are not "yes or no" questions. They are meant to be returned to again and again, as part of your own healing, learning, and growth as a practitioner.

Section 1: Examining Power and Position

When I walk into a room with Black clients, what assumptions do I carry about their intelligence, their choices, their pain, or their trust in me?

How has my own race, background, or privilege shaped the way I view addiction, recovery, or justice?

In what ways might my presence feel safe or unsafe, to a client with a history of being surveilled, punished, or pathologized?

Section 2: Language and Listening

Do I talk to clients, or with them?

Do I use clinical language to protect myself from emotional discomfort?

When a client challenges me, do I get defensive or do I get curious?

Section 3: Cultural Respect in Practice

How do I honor the intelligence and resourcefulness that Black clients have developed in the face of oppression?

Do I ever interpret cultural expression—anger, silence, directness—as pathology?

How do I adapt MI principles without erasing cultural truth?

Section 4: Repair and Accountability

When I get it wrong, do I own it? Out loud?

Do I have relationships with colleagues or mentors who can call me in when I miss the mark?

How do I center humility—not just competence—in my professional identity?

Section 5: Collective Responsibility

What am I doing to dismantle racism, not just in the room, but in the system I work in?

How do I support healing for my Black clients beyond individual sessions?

What legacy do I want to leave in this field?

Final Reflection

You don't need to have all the answers. But you do need to keep asking the questions.

When we pair Motivational Interviewing with cultural awareness, we don't just help people change, we help them reclaim their power.

Acknowledgments

This manual was not created in isolation. It stands on the shoulders of generations—of those who made a way when there was no way, who found healing in struggle, who showed us how to survive and still believe in our own transformation.

To the men and women I've sat with in treatment rooms, courtrooms, drop-in centers, and recovery circles you shaped this work. Your stories, your pain, your breakthroughs, and even your silence taught me more than any textbook ever could.

To every clinician, peer specialist, and street soldier trying to do right by our people—this manual is for you. Not because you need a script, but because you deserve tools that match the fire you bring into this work.

To my elders and ancestors—thank you for whispering wisdom when I almost lost my way. And to the next generation: may you find power in healing, truth in your voice, and purpose in your pain.

Final Notes

Motivational Interviewing for African Americans is more than a guide it's a challenge.

It's a challenge to the field to do better.It's a challenge to practitioners to listen deeper.It's a challenge to all of us to honor culture as sacred, not secondary.

We've talked about trauma—but also legacy. We've unpacked resistance but also resilience. We've reflected on language, but also power.

This manual doesn't pretend to be the final word. It's a beginning. A foundation. A call to action.

So whether you're a therapist, a counselor, a peer, a pastor, or someone who just gives a damn, let this be your charge:

Don't just use MI.Live it. Lead it. And adapt it with love.

Because our people are worth it.

– Kenneth Ginlack, LCSW, CSAC, ICS

Chapter 30
About The Author

Kenneth Ginlack, LCSW, CSAC, ICS, is a respected mental health and substance use professional, community leader, and advocate for culturally grounded care. He is the President and CEO of Serenity Inns Inc. and the Kenneth Ginlack Sr. Consulting and Training Center, where he leads initiatives that uplift Black men, support reentry populations, and transform behavioral health systems.

With over two decades of experience, Kenneth has worked at every level of the treatment and recovery field from direct service to executive leadership. He is known for his authentic and relatable approach to healing, rooted in lived experience, clinical excellence, and a deep commitment to justice.

Kenneth has trained professionals across the country in trauma-informed care, clinical supervision, and community-based recovery strategies. He serves on the Milwaukee County Mental Health Board, leads multiple nonprofit organizations, and was recognized as the 2023 Nonprofit Executive of the Year by BizTimes Milwaukee.

At the heart of his work is a belief that transformation is always possible and that culturally responsive care is not optional it is essential.

PART TWO

The Practitioner Workbook

Motivational Interviewing for African Americans

The Practitioner Workbook

Kenneth Ginlack, LCSW, CSAC, ICS

For permission requests, contact: kennginlack@gmail.com

ISBN: [To be assigned]
First Edition: 2025
Printed in the United States of America.

Motivational Interviewing for African Americans

The Practitioner Workbook

Kenneth Ginlack LCSW, CSAC, ICS

For permission requests, contact: **kennginlack@gmail.com**

Title: *Motivational Interviewing for African Americans: The Practitioner Workbook*
Author: Kenneth Ginlack, LCSW, CSAC, ICS
ISBN: [To be assigned]
First Edition: 2025

Printed in the United States of America.

Contents

1. Foreword 1
2. Acknowledgments 2
3. MI Is Not Magic. It Is Relationship 3
4. The Role of the Practitioner 6
5. Change Is Not a Straight Line! It's a Cultural Journey 10
6. Core Skills of Motivational Interviewing in Black Communities (OARS – Open Ended Questions, Affirmations, Reflections, Summaries) 13
7. The Four Core Processes of MI in Real Time 17
   Engaging. Focusing. Evoking. Planning.
   - Engaging: Trust Before Tools
   - Focusing: What Matters Most to Them
   - Evoking: Pulling the Truth Out, Not Pushing It In
   - Planning: Support Without Pressure
   - In Session (Facilitator Prompt – Optional)
8. Motivational Interviewing Under Pressure 22
   Court. CPS. Mandates. Survival.
9. Trauma Is in the Room Before You Are 26
   You are not just meeting the client. You are meeting their story.
10. Staying in the Work Without Losing Yourself 30
    Supervision, Support, and Survival for Practitioners
11. Structure That Holds, Not Pressures 33
    Facilitating Motivational Interviewing with Flexibility and Care

12. Closing Reflections 37
Keep the Work Human

13. Final Message 39

14. About the Author 40
Kenneth Ginlack, LCSW, CSAC, ICS

Chapter 1
Foreword

This workbook comes from years of sitting in rooms with people who have every reason not to trust. People who have been talked at, reported on, judged, and misunderstood. People who walk into sessions already knowing how to survive the system, but rarely feeling safe enough to speak their truth inside it.

It also comes from being a practitioner who was tired of feeling like the work was supposed to be scripted, controlled, or performed. I did not want a method that felt robotic. I needed something real. Something that left room for presence. For culture. For rhythm. For honesty.

Motivational Interviewing gave me a way to be both clinical and human. It let me bring my full self into the room, not just my credentials. But even MI has to be adapted to fit our people. Because we come with history. We come with deep protection. We come with stories that do not fit cleanly into stages of change.

This workbook is not meant to impress. It is meant to support. It is for the practitioner who wants to show up better. Who wants to ask better questions? Who wants to listen differently? And who wants to do all of that without losing their voice in the process?

You do not have to get this perfect. You just have to be present.

If this workbook helps you do that, even a little, then it did what it was supposed to do.

Chapter 2
Acknowledgments

This work is the result of years in the field, years in the struggle, and years in the healing.

To the people I have worked with over the years. In treatment centers. In community rooms. In court systems. In the quiet spaces where real change begins. Thank you for trusting me with your stories. Your experiences live in these pages.

To the men and women who showed up to the work with open hearts and unspoken pain. Your honesty shaped the way I listen and the way I lead.

To my colleagues and clinical mentors. You sharpened my skills and challenged me to bring both evidence and empathy into every room I walk into. You showed me that Motivational Interviewing is not just technique. It is presence. It is patience. It is partnership.

To the Black clinicians, peers, and community leaders who hold it down every day without always being seen or celebrated. Your wisdom is sacred. Your voice matters. I see you.

To my family. Your love has been my anchor. Thank you for standing beside me as I built this path. You are part of every page.

To God. I would not be here without grace. Recovery taught me how to live. Faith taught me how to serve. This work is my offering back.

To those who are new to this work and those who have walked it for years. May this workbook support your mission. May it speak your language. May it help you keep showing up when it would be easier to walk away.

Chapter 3
MI Is Not Magic. It Is Relationship

Big Idea

Some people get trained in Motivational Interviewing and think it is just a technique. A way to get people to say the right thing. To move faster. To behave better. But MI is not magic. It is not a shortcut. It is not a trick.

It is relationship.It is how you sit with someone without needing to fix them.
It is how you listen for what matters to them, not just what matters to the agency.
It is how you build something that is not based on power, but on presence.

If you do not have a real relationship, the method will not matter.
If the person does not feel safe, they will not go deep.
If they do not feel respected, they will not stay long.

This chapter is about slowing down. It is about remembering that the technique is only as strong as the trust it is built on.

Reflection Prompt

Think about a time when someone offered you solutions before they understood your story.

How did it feel ?

Did you trust them ?

Did you open up or shut down ?

____

____

____

____

Now think about a time when someone simply listened. No fixing. No diagnosing. Just presence.

How did that feel ?

What did it allow you to say or do?

What made it different?

Use this space to reflect:

Practice Exercise: Real Life MI

Motivational Interviewing uses four core processes. These are not steps to rush. They are relationship movements that unfold with trust.

1. Engaging – Building trust and safety. Without it, nothing works.

2. Focusing – Helping the person identify what matters most to them.

3. Evoking – Listening for their own reasons and readiness to change.

4. Planning – Supporting their next step when they are ready to name it.

Example

A young man came into group with arms crossed, court mandated, and silent. I welcomed him by name and thanked him for showing up. I did not pressure him to speak. I gave the room permission to hold him as he was. Three weeks later, he said he kept coming back because no one tried to force him to talk. That was engagement. That was Motivational Interviewing in practice before one skill was even used.

Use the space below to write your own example. Do not clean it up. Use your real voice.

____

____

____

____

Mirror Moment

I do not need to be fixed.

I need to be seen.

I need to be heard.

I need to be safe enough to say what I really want.

What comes up for you when you read those lines ?

What have you done to create that kind of safety for someone else ?

Where do you still need to grow ?

____

____

____

____

____

In Session Prompt (Facilitator Prompt – Optional)

Ask the practitioner group or individual:

What is the difference between being heard and being handled?

Let the space breathe. Do not rush the answer. Let the silence speak.

Use the space below to write what comes up in session.

____

____

____

____

____

Chapter 4
The Role of the Practitioner

Big Idea

Being a practitioner in Motivational Interviewing is not about being the expert in someone else's life. It is about learning how to show up fully without taking over. You are not here to fix or force. You are here to hold space with integrity, presence, and humility.

This role is not just technical. It is relational. It is emotional. And when working with Black clients, it is cultural. You are stepping into a space where people carry pain, power, history, and pressure. The question is not just what tools you bring. It is who you are when you walk into the room.

Practitioners who show up with their titles louder than their listening will miss the moment. This work demands more than credentials. It requires heart, respect, and self-awareness.

Reflection Prompt

When you are sitting across from someone in pain, what do you believe your role is?
Is it to solve?
To guide?
To listen?
To direct?

Write down what you *honestly* believe your role is — not what the manual says, but what your gut says.

____

____

Now reflect on this:

What do *your clients* think your role is?

Have you ever asked them?

Practice Exercise: Power Check

Think about a moment where you were in a position of authority – maybe you were running group, doing an assessment, or responding to a crisis.

Now ask yourself:

- Did I center the other person's voice or my own?
- Did I respond with curiosity or correction?
- Did I leave space for resistance without seeing it as disrespect?

Write about that moment here.

Example

A woman came into my office furious. She was told she had to complete this program or lose her housing. She did not want to be there and told me that directly. I could have pulled rank. I could have laid out the rules. Instead, I said, "You do not have to pretend to like this. I am not here to punish you. I am here if and when you are ready to use this space for yourself."

She stayed silent. Then she said, "You are the first person who didn't take my attitude personally."

That was the moment the work began. That was me choosing relationship over power.

Mirror Moment

Read these words out loud or to yourself:

"I cannot ask someone to trust me if I have not earned it."

Let that sit.

Now ask yourself:

How do I earn trust in my work?

Do I expect it to be given automatically?

Do I see resistance as disrespect or protection?

Write down what comes up.

____

____

____

____

In Session Prompt (Facilitator Prompt – Optional)

Ask the room:

What does it feel like when someone talks to you like they know everything about you after five minutes?

What does it feel like when someone actually takes the time to understand you before they speak?

Let the group talk. Let the stories come forward. Do not rush to wrap it up. Let them say what needs to be said.

Use the lines below to write what came up in your group or your own heart.

____

____

____

____

Chapter 5

Change Is Not a Straight Line! It's a Cultural Journey

Big Idea

The Stages of Change are often presented like a clean ladder: precontemplation, contemplation, preparation, action, maintenance. But change is not linear, and it sure is not clean.

In Black communities, change is shaped by trust, safety, history, and context. What may look like resistance is often protection. What may sound like denial could actually be survival. Practitioners who miss that will label people incorrectly and lose the moment.

Change takes time. And for many of our people, it also takes trust, community, and cultural belonging. If we do not understand that, we will treat behavior without understanding the burden beneath it.

Reflection Prompt

Think about a client or group member you worked with who did not seem ready to change.

What stage did you assume they were in?

Were they really resistant or were they protecting something?

Were they avoiding change or were they tired of being judged?

Write about that moment.

____

____

____

____

____

Now reflect on yourself:

When have you resisted change in your own life?

What was underneath that resistance?

Was it fear? Was it shame? Was it survival?

____

____

____

____

____

Example

A man in my group said, "I am not here for treatment. The judge sent me. I just need to finish this so I can stay out of jail."

A few years ago, I would have called that denial. I would have said he was not ready. But I asked one more question:

"When did people first start trying to fix you?"

He looked at me and said, "Since I was thirteen. I have been in courtrooms most of my life. No one ever asked me what I wanted. They just told me what I had to do."

That was not denial. That was exhaustion. That was someone surviving the system. He was not in precontemplation. He was in protest.

Once I honored that, he started to open up. He began to say what *he* wanted. Not just what he had to do to check a box.

That is where change began.

Mirror Moment

What does it mean to honor someone's resistance instead of breaking it down?

What would it look like to listen to the wisdom inside someone's ambivalence?

Write what this brings up for you. Be honest.

____

____

____

____

____

In Session (Facilitator Prompt – Optional)

Ask the group:

What does change look like when you do not feel safe enough to trust it yet?

What do you wish practitioners understood about what holds you back?

Give space for stories. Do not rush to the next topic. Let what is said sit in the room. Use the space below to write what you heard, or what you felt as the facilitator.

____

____

____

____

____

Chapter 6
Core Skills of Motivational Interviewing in Black Communities
(OARS – Open Ended Questions, Affirmations, Reflections, Summaries)

Big Idea

The skills of Motivational Interviewing are simple on paper but complex in practice. Open-ended questions. Affirmations. Reflections. Summaries. These are the core tools.

But in Black communities, how you use these tools matters as much as the tools themselves. You can ask an open-ended question and still sound like a detective. You can affirm someone and still sound performative. You can reflect and still sound like you are trying to sound clinical instead of being present.

OARS only work when they are delivered with real presence, cultural humility, and human rhythm. If they do not feel authentic, they do not build trust. And if they do not build trust, they do not work.

Reflection Prompt

Have you ever asked an open-ended question that felt scripted or forced?
What happened in the moment?
Did the client respond with trust, or did they shut down?

____

Think about a time you offered an affirmation.

Did it land as genuine, or did it feel like a checklist compliment?

What was the client's response?

Practice Exercise: OARS in Real Language

Take each letter in OARS and write down an example that would sound natural in your voice. Not in textbook language. In the language you would actually use in session.

O – Open-Ended Question

Example:

A – Affirmation

Example:

R – Reflection

Example:

____

____

____

S – Summary

Example:

____

____

____

Now ask yourself – would I say that if the client were my cousin, my brother, my mother, my son?

If not, rephrase it. Make it real.

Example

A client said, **"I haven't had a drink in three days."**

The clinician responded, "That's great progress. We can mark that down as early maintenance."

The client looked away. Disconnected.

Another practitioner stepped in and said,

"Three days? That's real. Most people have no idea what it takes just to get through one."

The client nodded. Then said, "This the first time I made it that long in months."

The first response rushed to a label. The second stayed with the person.

One quoted a stage. The other made space.

That is the difference.

Mirror Moment

What kind of language do you use when you are nervous or unsure in session?

Do you fall back on clinical talk?

Do you rely on the script?

How do you know when you are really showing up and not just performing your role?

Write your truth.

____

____

____

____

____

In Session (Facilitator Prompt – Optional)

Ask the room:

When has someone said the right thing the wrong way?

How do you know when someone's words are real versus rehearsed?

Let the room open up. Do not jump in to fix or reframe.

Write down what came up in the group or in you.

____

____

____

____

____

Chapter 7
The Four Core Processes of MI in Real Time
Engaging. Focusing. Evoking. Planning.

Big Idea

Motivational Interviewing is not just a technique. It is a rhythm. A way of moving with someone instead of at them.

The four core processes – Engaging, Focusing, Evoking, and Planning – are not boxes to check. They are not steps in a staircase. They are movements in a relationship. You shift into each one based on the person in front of you, not the manual in your head.

In Black communities, this rhythm has extra weight. People do not show up already trusting you. They may carry history, fear, fatigue, or quiet. You have to earn the space you stand in. These processes are not about control. They are about respect. They are about listening and letting the work unfold from there.

Engaging: Trust Before Tools

Description

This is the beginning. If trust is not present, nothing else works. Engaging means showing up in a way that says, "You are safe here." Not just through words, but through tone, energy, posture, and patience.

Reflection Prompt

When you meet a new client, what do you say or do to build trust?
What do you avoid doing so it does not feel like intake or interrogation?

____

____

____

____

____

Example

A young woman sat in the back of group with her hoodie up and arms folded. I did not call her out. I did not make her check in. I simply said, "Glad you made it." No pressure. No spotlight.

Two sessions later, she said,

"Y'all didn't force me to talk. That's why I came back."

That was Engaging.

Focusing: What Matters Most to Them

Description

Focusing is not about narrowing someone into your agenda. It is about helping them name what matters most to them. It is about clarity. Not control.

Reflection Prompt

Have you ever brought your own agenda into a session?

Did you push too hard or try to steer too early?

How do you slow down and let their focus come forward?

____

____

____

____

____

Practice Exercise

What is one question you could ask to help someone define what matters to them? Use your own voice. No assumptions. Just space.

____

____

____

____

____

Example

A client kept talking about his court case. I asked, "What do you want from all this?" He said, "I want people to stop watching me like I am about to fail."

That was his focus. Not sobriety. Not steps. Safety.

Evoking: Pulling the Truth Out, Not Pushing It In

Description

Evoking is helping someone find their own voice. Their reason. Their why. It is not about you convincing them. It is about listening so well that they hear themselves more clearly.

Reflection Prompt

Think of a time someone told you what you should do.

Did it help you change, or did it shut you down?

Now flip it. How often do you do that in session?

____

____

____

____

____

Example

I asked a man, "What is keeping you coming back to group?"

He said, "Honestly it is not even the group. My son asked me if I was going to be around this year."

That was his reason. Not the treatment plan. Not the court. His child.

That was Evoking.

Planning: Support Without Pressure

Description

Planning comes when someone is ready. Not when we are ready. It is not about rushing people into change. It is about walking beside them once they name what they want.

Reflection Prompt

Have you ever rushed someone into a goal because you felt like you had to do something?

What happened?

How would it have felt to wait and let them lead?

____

____

____

____

____

Practice Exercise

What is one question you could ask someone who seems ready to take a step, but needs it to be on their own terms?

____

____

____

____

____

Example

A client said, "I guess I should stop smoking weed so I can pass this drug test for a job, right?"

I said, "What do you think you are actually ready for?"

He said, "I am not saying I am ready to quit, but I could chill out long enough to pass the test and get to work."

We talked about what that could look like. What it might take.

That became the plan.

Not mine. His.

That is Planning.

In Session (Facilitator Prompt – Optional)

Ask the group:

Which one of the four MI processes is hardest for you to sit in?

Which one do you rush? Which one do you avoid? Why?

Let the room breathe.

Let them talk honestly about what makes certain stages uncomfortable or unfamiliar.

Do not over-teach. Just listen.

Use the space below to reflect on what came up in the group or in yourself.

____

____

____

____

____

Chapter 8
Motivational Interviewing Under Pressure
Court. CPS. Mandates. Survival.

Big Idea

Sometimes people walk into the room not because they want to be there but because someone told them they had to. A judge. A probation officer. A CPS worker. A system. That pressure shows up before they even sit down. You can feel it in the way they breathe. The way they fold their arms. The way they look at you like you are part of the same machine that is watching them.

Motivational Interviewing is not just for voluntary clients. It is not just for the people who show up open and ready to grow. It works best when the walls are already up. When trust has to be earned. When people feel trapped. That is where MI lives.

This chapter is about how to show up without forcing. How to listen without defending the system. How to let people be mad, be guarded, be real and still know they are safe with you.

Reflection Prompt

Think about a time when someone came into your group or session because they had to.

Did you treat them the same way you treat someone who came in on their own?

Did you try to earn their trust, or did you expect it?

____

____

____

____

____

Example – Probation

A client came in talking fast. He had just seen his PO the day before.

He said,

"She said I haven't been showing up to group. If I miss one more time, she locking me up. I am here but I am not saying shit so mark me here. Go report that."

I did not push. I did not try to make him talk.

I said,

"Cool. You are here. If all you do today is sit and breathe, that counts."

He stayed quiet for a while.

Then he said,

"I ain't trippin no more. I was just upset. But on the real, I was absent. My girl was in the hospital and I had to watch the kids. I know you understand. You never treated me like a criminal."

That was not him getting compliant.

That was him getting honest.

That was Motivational Interviewing working under pressure, not performance.

Example – CPS

A woman came in for her first session after a CPS referral.

She sat down and said,

"All of y'all work together trying to take my kids. So don't ask me nothing personal about my house."

I said,

"It's all good. You do not have to say nothing you do not feel comfortable saying. I am here for you. I am a part of the system, but I do not work for the system. I work for you.

I am here to help you in whatever way you need me to be. You do not have to share anything until it feels right to you. This space is yours, not theirs."

She paused. Then she said,

"You different. The rest of them fake friendly. You just real."

That was not trust handed over. That was trust earned.

That is what MI looks like in a system that already feels like punishment.

Mirror Moment

Ask yourself:

When someone walks in mad, guarded, or silent, do you take it personal?

Do you push to prove you are different, or do you give space for them to find out on their own?

Are you showing up with presence or with pressure?

Write what comes up.

____

____

____

____

____

In Session (Facilitator Prompt – Optional)

Ask the group:

What does it feel like when someone walks in because the court or CPS made them come?

How do you avoid becoming part of that system energy?

How does MI let people keep their voice even when the system tries to take it?

Let the room breathe. Let people speak the truth.

Write what stood out.

____

Chapter 9

Trauma Is in the Room Before You Are

You are not just meeting the client. You are meeting their story.

Big Idea

Trauma is not always loud. Sometimes it walks in quiet. Arms folded. Eyes low. Voice tight.

Sometimes trauma looks like disrespect but it is protection.
Sometimes it sounds like attitude but it is history.
Sometimes it shows up before a single word is spoken.

And if we are not listening, we will miss it.

In Black communities, trauma is layered. It comes from violence, poverty, grief, school systems, justice systems, and sometimes our own homes. But it also comes from generations of being watched, silenced, removed, and labeled. So when a client steps into your space with tension, with anger, or with nothing to say at all , you are not just meeting that moment. You are meeting everything they have been through that brought them to that moment.

And for some clients, trust is not broken. It was never there to begin with. You have to earn it, not through what you say, but how you show up. That is where Motivational Interviewing matters most. When pressure is high. When trust is low. When survival is leading.

Reflection Prompt

Think of a time a client pulled away from you emotionally or went completely silent.
Did you see it as disrespect or as something deeper?
How did you respond?

____

____

____

____

____

Example – He Was Not Angry. He Was Hurt.

A young man in group barely spoke. I asked him a question and he fired back:
"Why you asking me all this? You just gonna write it down and use it later."

I did not correct him. I did not explain. I just said,

"You sound like somebody who has been through some shit."

He looked at me for the first time and said,

"Finally. Somebody gets it."

That was not attitude. That was trauma that had not been named yet.

Example – The Pen and the Police

A woman sat across from me during intake. I started writing while she spoke.

She said,

"Everything I say, you write it down like the police. That's why I don't talk. People use my words to hurt me."

She had trusted someone once and it cost her.
A counselor reported what she said. CPS got involved.
She lost her home. Her siblings were taken.

I said,

"I can put the pen down and we can just talk openly if that works better for you."

She didn't open up that day. But she stayed.
That was a start.

Example – Trust Has Been Gone

Another client said,

"No man ever helped me. They either left or used me. So why should I trust you?"

And a young woman told me,

"Black women don't expect Black men to show up for them. Not now. They never could protect us."

That was not attitude. That was grief. That was truth. That was experience.

When a client says, "I don't trust this," what they are really saying is:

"I've been let down before and I'm not doing that again."

That is not resistance. That is self-protection.

Mirror Moment

Ask yourself:

When trauma shows up in your room, do you try to fix it or do you try to hold it?

Do you ask questions that make space – or do you close in on the problem?

What does your presence say when your words are not enough?

Write your truth.

____

____

____

____

____

In Session (Facilitator Prompt – Optional)

Ask the group:

What does trauma sound like in the rooms you sit in?

What does it look like when someone has been let down by every helping hand that said

it was safe?

How does MI let us slow down instead of pushing forward when a client is not ready?

Let the group speak freely. Hold space. No rush.

Write down what came up.

____

____

____

____

____

Chapter 10
Staying in the Work Without Losing Yourself
Supervision, Support, and Survival for Practitioners

Big Idea

Motivational Interviewing is not just a method. It is a way of showing up. But showing up day after day in systems that are under-resourced, in rooms full of trauma, and in jobs that ask more than they give, takes something real.

This chapter is about the part of the work people do not always talk about.

You are the one running groups, holding space, training staff, writing reports, and still expected to stay calm when the room gets hot. Some days you are holding the stories of others while no one is asking how your story is doing.

Supervision is supposed to help. But sometimes it turns into paperwork. Or performance. Or pressure.

What you need is reflection. Space. Support that sees the full you.

MI asks us to show up with presence. You cannot do that if no one is holding space for you. This chapter is about what it takes to stay in the work without burning out, breaking down, or building walls.

When was the last time you felt truly supported in your work?

Not tolerated. Not managed. Supported.

What did that support look like? Who made it possible?

____

____

____

____

____

Example – Peer Support, Not Performance Review

I had a session that hit me hard. The client said something that brought up my own pain. I stayed professional in the moment, but I carried it home. It stayed with me.

I called a peer. Someone who has done this work. Not a supervisor. Not someone checking boxes. Just someone who gets it.

I said,

"That session got to me. I kept it together, but it landed deeper than I expected."

They said,

"You held space for them. Now who is holding space for you."

That was what I needed. Not an evaluation. Not advice. Just care.

That is what support can sound like.

Example – I Do Not Need a Flyer

A practitioner once said,

"I do not need a self-care flyer. I need a break. I need someone to check on me who is not asking for a note or a chart. I need to be able to say I am tired without someone putting that in my file."

Sometimes the pressure is not just the work.

It is the way we are expected to carry it without cracking.

But healing work cracks us if we do not have space to be whole.

MI is about presence. That presence has to include you too.

Mirror Moment

Ask yourself:

When do you check in on your own energy, not as a professional but as a person?

Who do you talk to when the work hits something personal in you?
What does real support look like for you?

____

____

____

____

____

In Session (Facilitator Prompt – Optional)

Ask the group:

What do you do when the work starts to wear you down?

Who do you trust enough to say, "I am not okay," without fear of judgment or consequence?

What would it look like to build a culture of care, not just compliance?

Let people speak honestly. No fixing. No performing. Just reflection.

Write what stood out.

____

____

____

____

____

Chapter 11

Structure That Holds, Not Pressures

Facilitating Motivational Interviewing with Flexibility and Care

Big Idea

Some people think structure and freedom do not mix. But in Motivational Interviewing, the right kind of structure creates more freedom not less.

Clients need space to breathe, but they also need something that can hold them. Something that does not push, but guides. Something that does not control, but anchors. That is what MI offers when it is done right. It gives the room shape without squeezing out the voice of the person inside it.

As a facilitator, your role is not to run a perfect group. Your role is to open space. Your tools are not just worksheets and topics. Your tools are curiosity, presence, and the ability to meet the room where it is.

This chapter offers ways to bring MI into group work, peer sessions, or one on ones using exercises that invite honesty and give people control over their own process.

Reflection Prompt

Think about a time you ran a group or session that felt too tight or too loose.
What did it need more of? What did it need less of?

____

____

____

Example – A Group Without Pressure

A young man came into group with arms crossed, court mandated, and silent. I welcomed him by name and thanked him for showing up. I did not pressure him to speak. I let the room hold him without pushing.

Three weeks later, he said,

"I kept coming back because no one forced me to talk."

That was engagement.

That was MI in practice before any technique was even used.

Facilitator Exercise – I Do Not Need to Be Fixed

Write these four lines on the board or read them out loud:

I do not need to be fixed

I need to be seen

I need to be heard

I need to be safe enough to say what I really want

Then ask the group:

- What comes up for you when you hear those lines?
- Where have you felt safe enough to speak freely?
- What does it take for someone to actually feel heard?

Let people write, speak, or sit in silence. Give space.

In Session Prompt – Real Voices, Not Just Scripts

Ask the room:

What kind of language do you use when you are nervous or unsure in session?

Do you fall back on clinical talk? Do you perform your role or do you show up as yourself?

Let the answers be messy. That is where the truth lives.

____

____

____

____

____

Try This – OARS In Your Own Language

Take the four core MI tools – Open Questions, Affirmations, Reflections, and Summaries – and have the group translate them into language that sounds natural.

Write each on the board and ask:

- **Open Questions:** What would this sound like in your voice, not the textbook?
  Example: "What made today harder than usual?"

- **Affirmations:** What is a real way you would affirm someone without sounding like a poster?
  Example: "You have really been holding a lot and you are still standing."

- **Reflections:** How do you reflect without parroting or sounding clinical?
  Example: "It sounds like you are not sure who to trust with this."

- **Summaries:** How do you wrap up what you have heard in a way that respects their story?
  Example: "So far you have shared anger, exhaustion, and a real desire to do better. Did I get that right?"

Let practitioners practice these in pairs or as a group. The goal is not perfection. The goal is presence.

Mirror Moment

Ask yourself:
When I run groups or sessions, am I present or am I performing?
Do I use language that invites trust – or that protects me from risk?
What do I need to unlearn so that I can show up more fully?

____

____

____

____

____

Chapter 12

Closing Reflections

Keep the Work Human

Big Idea

You made it through this workbook. You read the stories, answered the hard questions, and hopefully saw some of yourself on these pages.

But before you go, let's be clear — this is not the end of anything. This is just a reminder.

A reminder that MI is not about being perfect. It is about being present.

It is not about knowing all the right moves. It is about noticing when to stop talking.

It is not about fixing people. It is about respecting the part of them that already knows.

If you do not remember anything else from this workbook, remember this:

Presence is your power.

Curiosity is your tool.

Relationship is the real work.

This is not just technique. It is care. It is attention. It is you, showing up over and over again — not with answers, but with space. Not with control, but with trust.

That is the work. And that is enough.

Reflection Prompt

What do you want to carry forward from this workbook into your next session?

What part of you got clearer during this process?

What will you leave behind?

____

____

____

____

____

Mirror Moment

Ask yourself:

Why did I choose this work?

Who am I doing it for?

What keeps me grounded when the room gets heavy?

____

____

____

____

____

This is your reminder:

You are not just delivering services.

You are offering presence.

And when it is done with honesty and care, that is the intervention.

Chapter 13
Final Message

Thank you for being here. For doing this work. For sitting in hard rooms with people who are carrying more than they can say out loud.

This workbook was created for practitioners who are tired of checkboxes and systems that talk about healing but do not make space for it. It was built for people who want to show up with presence, not just technique.

Motivational Interviewing is not magic. It is relationship.
It is not a script. It is trust built slowly.
And it is not about being perfect. It is about being real, even when the room is heavy.

If anything in this workbook helped you slow down, reflect, or come back to why you do this work then it did its job.

Stay rooted. Stay present. Stay human.
And never forget **you are not just doing the work. You are part of the healing.**

Kenneth Ginlack, LCSW, CSAC, ICS

Chapter 14

About the Author

Kenneth Ginlack, LCSW, CSAC, ICS

Kenneth Ginlack is a Licensed Clinical Social Worker, Clinical Substance Abuse Counselor, and Independent Clinical Supervisor with over 17 years in recovery. He brings deep experience from treatment centers, community programs, and justice systems. Kenneth has spent his career serving clients and training practitioners to lead with presence, respect, and realness.

He has facilitated thousands of groups and developed culturally responsive training models rooted in trauma awareness, motivational interviewing, and lived experience.

His work does not come from theory alone. It comes from years of sitting in hard rooms, walking alongside clients, and knowing what it means to be both the helper and the one healing.

Kenneth is the founder of multiple training initiatives for clinicians working with African American populations and has become a trusted voice for those doing the real work in complex systems.

This workbook is not just something he wrote. It is something he lived.

References

Miller, W. R., & Rollnick, S. (2013). Motivational interviewing: Helping people change (3rd ed.). Guilford Press.

Miller, W. R., & Rollnick, S. (2023). Motivational interviewing: Helping people change and grow (4th ed.). Guilford Press.

Rollnick, S., Miller, W. R., & Butler, C. C. (2008). Motivational interviewing in health care: Helping patients change behavior. Guilford Press.

Sue, D. W., & Sue, D. (2016). Counseling the culturally diverse: Theory and practice (7th ed.). Wiley.

Tervalon, M., & Murray-García, J. (1998). Cultural humility versus cultural competence: A critical distinction in defining physician training outcomes in multicultural education. Journal of Health Care for the Poor and Underserved, 9(2), 117–125. https://doi.org/10.1353/hpu.2010.0233

Van Dernoot Lipsky, L. (2009). Trauma stewardship: An everyday guide to caring for self while caring for others. Berrett-Koehler.

Watkins, M., & Shulman, H. (2008). Toward psychologies of liberation. Palgrave Macmillan.

www.ingramcontent.com/pod-product-compliance
Lightning Source LLC
LaVergne TN
LVHW082344200926
848481LV00012B/3448
9798218726782